Parenting

Parenting
The Long Journey

by Joe Rich

BICENTENNIAL

1807

WILEY

2007

BICENTENNIAL

John Wiley & Sons Canada, Ltd.

National Library of Canada Cataloguing in Publication Data

Rich, Joe (Joe Charles)
   Parenting : the long journey / Joe Rich.
Includes index.
ISBN-13 978-0-470-83923-2
ISBN-10 0-470-83923-6
   1. Parenting. 2. Child rearing. I. Title.
HQ769.M5318 2006   649.1   C2006-902722-6

Production Credits:
Cover design: Ian Koo
Interior text design: Tegan Wallace
Cover photographer: Lorella Zanetti
Anniversary logo design: Richard Pacifico
Printer: Printcrafters

John Wiley & Sons Canada, Ltd.
6045 Freemont Blvd.
Mississauga, Ontario
L5R 4J3

Printed in Canada

1 2 3 4 5 PC 10 09 08 07 06

For
Brenda
Alysse, Devra and Leora

As it turns out,
watching great parenting every day
does make it easier to write about it…

Contents

Foreword by Marilyn Denis

I'm no psychic, but something tells me right now you're stand-ing in a bookstore contemplating whether or not to purchase this particular item, and you're hoping the foreword will tip the scale one way or the other. For those of you who have watched him on CityLine, Joe Rich needs no introduction; you may proceed straight to the check-out counter, thank-you! For those that haven't, I want you to know that **Joe Rich is my parenting mentor**. And I'll bet that after you read *Parenting: The Long Journey,* you'll reach for it again and again every time you get into a parenting snag. And beware! Friends are going to ask to borrow this book!

So, who will want to read this book, anyway?

Parents, obviously, and grandparents. Even if you don't yet have kids but are having fun trying, you'll want to read this book. You'll want to read this book if you've tried to apply old parenting standards and can't figure out why they don't work today. You'll want to read this book if you're wondering when it's the right time for kids to do their own laundry, or the right time for them to stay home alone, or the right time for you to bite your tongue when the sight of their room gives you nightmares! You'll want to read this book if your child tells you he or she feels a certain way and you're not sure how to respond. You'll want to read this book if you own a computer.

Oh, there's more!

You'll want to read this book if you can't wait for your kids to leave home, or if you suspect they feel the same way! You'll want to read this book if you've always thought you're doing okay as a parent only to suddenly realize you're not doing okay at all. (Remember, it's never too late.) You'll want to read this book if you've ever felt confused about how to handle a situation, or if you can't decide whether you're a parent or an unpaid babysitter. And if you think that parenting ends when kids turn 18, you'd better read this book before leaving the store!

When you need an answer straight away, it's right here in this book.

When I run into any parenting issue I always think to myself, *What would Joe say? What would Joe do?* Joe Rich's parenting advice is cut-and-dried and direct. He gives you the tools along with advice on how to use them to get the best results.

Parenting is more than just the biggest job you are ever going to have. Consider it your lifelong *dream* job. You get one chance. And Joe Rich can help make sure you enjoy it!

Marilyn Denis

Acknowledgements

I am grateful to all those who have come to my assistance in cheering me on or in providing hands-on expertise in the writing of this book. Special mention needs to be made of the following:

- Leah Fairbank, whose editorial excellence was invaluable as I navigated my way through the process, with Jennifer Smith at the helm along with all of the Wiley staff who have come to my assistance throughout.

- Rickie Glickman, who was helpful at the start in inspiring the framework for the book as a community presentation for parents.

- Aimee Israel of LifeSpeak, who gave the push to get the written manuscript to John Wiley and Sons.

- Martyn Krys of FilmLegals, who helped to get things settled and in place.

- Marilyn Denis, for writing the foreword to the book and who over the years has been of invaluable assistance in my professional life and a good friend.

- Debra Feldman Pottens, for helping me to understand the ins and outs of the world of the media and for her helpful advice regarding marketing.

- Scott Wiseman (a.ka. The Webmaster) for his assistance in helping me navigate the Web and the Web site for all of these years.

- Deena Mandell for her ongoing support and wisdom as a colleague, professional partner and friend.

And then there is the host of friends, family and colleagues who are too numerous to mention but who collectively have a place in my heart and in these pages.

My sincerest thanks to one and all.

Introduction

Welcome to
Parenting: The Long Journey

Twenty-five years' experience of coaching, public speaking, leading parenting groups and working as a relationship expert has led me to identify the very best of parenting techniques, strategies and skills. My goal has always been the same, regardless of forum or medium: to help parents improve their respective parent–child relationships with ideas, advice and strategies that will offer insight and build parenting skills on an ongoing basis. The synthesis of these years of research and discovery are presented to you in this book, in the hope that you will discover, not how parenting *should look*, but a unique, courageous and joyful way of *looking at* parenting.

The challenges for today's parents range from the perennial problems of yelling, chores and homework to the more serious issues of building self-esteem and raising children to be healthy and independent adults. This book is designed to help parents develop the attitudes and skills they need to navigate through all these issues successfully. There are problem-solving techniques for each age and stage of your child's development, so keep the book handy for quick reference as your family changes and grows.

How is *looking at parenting* different from *how parenting should look*? Learning to develop positive and healthy perspectives on parenting encourages you to drop the quest for the perfect family. Instead, it shows you how you can combine contemporary and traditional parenting, how to recognize, accept and learn from your mistakes, and how to keep getting better, at every step along the journey. You'll discover how to say no and mean it, how to recharge your batteries—and how to maintain your love life!

The "ideal" family experience makes for a frustrating and unrealistic goal, and one that adds unnecessary pressure to the already demanding and unique challenges faced by today's parents. Parenting is a relationship. It isn't a job, or something we as parents "do" when we are at home with our kids. Although the word parenting suggests that it is a verb, conjuring up ideas like feeding, driving, disciplining and so on, it is in fact a noun, a relationship that involves growth, understanding and closeness for all parties. The focus of this book, then, is the notion that parenting is a symbiotic relationship, rather than a series of unpredictable highs and lows. It is not a storm to be weathered—it is a road to drive along.

You can use this book to help you explore the boundaries, definitions and truths of your current parent–child relationship(s), and to draw from your own experience as a parent in order to alter, strengthen or modify the basic principles it lays out. You'll be asked to consider endless relationship variables throughout the book, such as the history of your child's birth or entry into the family, issues of gender, the family constellation the parenting takes place in (step-family, nuclear family, single family, etc.) and developmental stages, to name but a few.

In Part I you'll find key concepts that will introduce you to a brand new set of parenting tools. These tools will be helpful to you in reading the next sections in the book (and in life!). Some of the skills can be put into practice the day you read about them, while others are designed to be phased in over longer periods of time. These practical suggestions will help you create a healthier parent–child relationship by encouraging you to think in terms of new attitudes and approaches when it comes to parenting your children.

Part II will prepare you for the journey ahead, no matter where you are in your own parenting adventure! You'll discover the skills and philosophies you need to be able to relax and enjoy your relationships with your children. *What to Pack* will coach you through your present day's dilemma and prepare you for what you are about to find on the road ahead. By the time you're through the section, you'll be looking at the map, the booster cables and the whistle in a whole new light! Think of it as an ounce of prevention and a lot of "cure-for-what-ails-you" as a parent today.

Part III contains fourteen essential lessons that combine everything you've learned so far about relationships, illustrated with real-world examples of parenting slip-ups and expert solutions. This section offers creative, effective suggestions and tips for healthy disciplining, spotting problems before they arise, encouraging leadership, raising independent children, kid-proofing your computer and much more.

Ultimately, this is a book to help you on the journey of parenting. It is about attitude, outlook and real life. It will help get you through all kinds of troublesome parenting traps, while maintaining your own steady course. It is about the everyday of parenting, with lots of helpful and insightful suggestions that can assist you with everything from the mundane task of saying no to how to get through some of those awful moments when you're sure you've lost it, turned into your own mother or father, and just can't remember which direction to head in or how to get there! The suggestions in this book emphasize the importance of building relationships that are marked by your participation and your efforts in being there for your children and for yourself. There are ways you can create positive changes in your parenting, no matter how well you are already doing. This is a book that will help to get you there.

Part I

Nine Keys to Phenomenal Parenting

You need keys to drive, and these first chapters will give you just that. Really great parenting hinges on these underlying ideas and principles, so I encourage you to begin exploring them here. You'll read about them in this first section and bump into them throughout the book as they are used to illustrate examples along the way. I begin here with "the parent as expert," and from this key point the others will flow.

Chapter One

The Parent as Expert

The easiest job in the world is to raise
someone else's children.

As you know, there are many experts on parenting. There are psychologists, social workers, teachers, celebrities, doctors and guidance counselors. They come to you on television, in magazines and electronically, as speakers and presenters and book writers and so on. They all have opinions and ideas about how to parent your children. Sometimes they are even disguised as the pushy mom in the school hallway that you're forced to listen to while you wait for your children.

As the saying above implies, it is easy to say what you would do with someone else's child, or how they should behave, but the truth is, raising your own—well, that's another story!

For a book about relationships to be helpful, including this one focused on the parent–child relationship, the author needs to remember where the expert's expertise ends and where the parent's expertise begins. Yes, I am an expert and I hope that my expertise will surface through suggestions, ideas, thoughts and encouragements as you read and think your way through this book. However, your expertise already exists, and it is extremely important in the application of this book—and of any other materials you use to aid your parent–child relationship.

**REST AREA
1 MILE**

Suggestions for your parenting need to be partnered with your own existing expertise. Never underestimate this fact.

Take a moment to identify your specific areas of expertise. For example, keep in mind that, to name only a few, you are an expert on:

- Your own life

- Your family and its history: likes, dislikes, dynamics and participants

- Your child or children and their individual traits, personalities and characteristics

- Recent and past events that affect your life, and how and when any good advice should be implemented

- Your personal goals and challenges in your parenting

- Your adult relationships and couple relationship

- Your culture

A parent of twins may not be the expert on all twins, but will certainly be the expert on *their* twins. In the same way, while the parent of a child with a handicap is likely well versed on the condition of the handicap, they truly are the leading world authority on their own child.

Sometimes parents are afraid to assert this expertise or to identify areas in their own life where it makes sense for them to be the expert. This is especially true when they are in the company of professionals. However, that is the very time when the expertise of the parent is most needed. External, objective advice in combination with the specific knowledge of the parent always works best!

In today's world of more complex family constellations (the step-family, reconstituted family, dual income family, bi-nuclear family), it is especially important for parents to be experts on their own lives; they must be able to give direction as well as take direction in meaningful and applicable ways. For example, a biological parent can be encouraged to confront situations and deal with them as they take place, whereas a new step-parent in the same situation would be advised to hang back, let things move a bit more slowly, and consider many more variables and possible outcomes before intervening on a parenting matter.

This book has been written keeping these varying constellations in mind, and the tools (such as "choosing your mode of transportation," or "thinking long") will be relevant to all parents, but especially useful to those who are willing to embrace their own expert status—in regard to their family and to themselves.

As you read along and discover ideas you'd like to try, I hope you'll use your expertise to make the ideas "fit," to alter them to suit *your* family situation.

REST AREA
1 MILE

Good advice and suggestions are like a nice suit hanging on the rack: just what many are looking for, but needing to be tailored and altered to fit the individual.

Start with Your Strengths

People generally begin to examine their parenting because something is going wrong. Because of this, it is important to begin to make positive changes in your parenting style from a position of strength.

Think for a moment about your own expertise and success as a parent. As easy as this sounds, it will probably take you at least a few moments to alter your mindset and get to your successes. So, think—what are you good at? Can you name a few things you are doing well? Is this one of those days or moments when you're feeling so low about how you're doing as a parent that you can't think of any successes at all? If it is, then you won't find what you are looking for here or anywhere else—yet! You must use your strengths to tackle the areas you want to improve upon in parenting

Finding Your Strengths

Here are some easy tips to help you remember all of the valuable, great work you do every day as a parent:

- Look at all areas of parenting in your search for strengths, from routines you do morning, noon and night (and in the middle of the night!) to special occasions and how you make them significant.

- Consider the things you *do* as a parent that are working well.

- Consider the things you *don't do* that you know wouldn't work.

- Think about what your children would say if you asked them what you are good at, and put those things on the list, too.

Okay, now you have a few strengths in mind. Maybe you made cookies today with the kids and realized you're the parent who does fun activities. You let the six-year-old wear what she wanted and avoided a battle over nothing. You promised you wouldn't yell all weekend and you didn't. You gave your four-year-old a little "mommy and me time" instead of watching your favorite show. You coach hockey. You read to your kids every day. You hug a lot.

Those are your strengths. Start your search for better parenting from this position, always. Train yourself to put a list of strengths in place just before you start searching for any improvements. Make this a base to start out from.

When you hear yourself say things like "I wish I didn't do that—I have to stop myself" or "Wow, she's such a great parent—I wish I was like that" . . .

STOP

Remind yourself of what you are good at.

Then take a look at what you'd specifically like to improve on.

Then consider how to make the improvement.

Everyone has doubts, room for improvement, successes and strengths. No one is *not good* at everything. It just isn't possible.

Here's how things look to Yolanda when she tries to start from a position of strengths:

> Yolanda is the mother of a three-year-old boy and a six-month-old baby girl. On most days Yolanda is over-tired. She is tired because she has an infant. She is over-tired (and upset) because her three-year-old comes into her bed every night. When she talks about this issue (to anyone) it is clear she feels she is a "failure" and that she is not doing what she should. Her focus on this is quite negative and the issue has grown larger in her mind than it may really be.

When asked to begin the helping process with the surprising question "What five things are you already good at?" she can't respond. With a little coaching and a few examples, she is able to come up with the following list of things she is already succeeding at as a parent:

1. Getting the three-year-old to eat food at the table.

2. Not taking things out on the kids when I'm upset.

3. Making sure the baby is healthy and gaining weight.

4. Trying hard to get out of the house with both kids for play times.

5. Taking one night a week to get out with friends.

Once Yolanda answers the question, she is ready to participate in hearing and integrating suggestions about the three-year-old and where he sleeps. She renews the knowledge that she has had some successes already and, in identifying what she is good at, she presents herself as an expert on her family. The shift towards seeing herself in a more positive and balanced way begins to take place before "solving the sleep issue." Now she can take her past successes with her into the process of dealing with the issues at hand.

Renewing your successes can be helpful at all points along the road of parenting. In fact, it is quite refreshing to hear someone speak in these terms: "Oh, I'm good at getting them to activities, but I'm working on saying no to treats on the way." In acknowledging the balance between what we are good at and what still needs some work, we are able to keep things in perspective and avoid getting lost in the negative.

Think of five things you are good at in parenting. The time will come when things aren't going so well, and you'll be glad you made the list in advance to help you balance things out as you seek change or improvement.

Chapter Two

"Better"

As parents, we're all aiming for the same thing. I like to call this "better." Aiming for better is a key concept you will need to understand in order to start and support your parenting journey.

> **REST AREA**
> **1 MILE**
>
> No matter what kind of job you're doing as parent on a particular day, everyone can do better.

One of the first tasks in shooting for better is to forget about perfect. Perfect is not better at its best! Perfect in anything to do with people and relationships (family, parenting, step-parenting, marriage) is a set-up for failure. If you shoot for the center of this target, you'll never hit it: perfect is a constantly moving target. You shoot, it moves.

Let that go! If this is how you measure yourself and others (*How close to perfect are they? How close am I? How about our relationship?*) nothing you do will ever be good enough. Perfect is the three young kids and the house that is so clean you can eat off the floor. Perfect is "we *never* fight." Perfect is "our children don't swear." Perfect is always on time, or always only "eating healthy." Perfect can create an awful lot of pressure, especially if you measure the daily events and relationship moments of your life against it.

It is also important not to let yourself hide behind the illusion that aiming for perfect means you have higher standards than others. People who aim for better also have high standards, and in addition, they experience a greater sense of success and accomplishment at steps along the path of change and improvement. Out with perfect and in with better!

In parenting, this is one idea you'll be glad you adopted. The idea of better works for everyone and can be applied to every relationship in a non-threatening and non-judgmental way. Parents may want to look at better in their parenting when they are actually in the middle of doing a fairly good job. They are in search of better in the form of new suggestions, objective input on their strategies, and skills appropriate to their child's new developmental stage. For others, aiming for better instead of perfect will make new-found struggles a lot easier, and lead to more positive feelings about the gains being made.

REST AREA
1 MILE

Putting better into practice will often mean changing *your* behaviors and attitudes along the way. For example, to get to better you'll have to stop saying, "What am I doing wrong?" and start saying, "How could I do this better?"

Better is always just a bit ahead of where you are. Better is accessible. Better is a reasonable target every day. Better is an idea that can help you find ways to encourage yourself as a parent.

Sometimes Getting to Better Means Getting to Okay

There will be points on the journey where a parent is naturally skilled, and points that require more conscious effort. At these more difficult spots your goal is simply to be "okay" until a developmental stage moves on or a series of events has passed you by. We'd all like to be great at parenting every stage of development. However, being great at everything would be trying to be perfect, not a realistic goal at all! At other points you will experience times when your parenting is going well, you'll continue to work at "better" and occasionally you will get to "great."

When parenting at those good-enough times, you could feel discouraged, lose confidence, or begin to see your co-parent as the better parent. It is important to try to remember that this is not a race or a competition and that you can focus on better; this is designed to help you feel good and move forward again. Try to keep in mind that this is *your* life. This is your family. These are your children. There is nothing to prove in all of this. This is about doing better in your life—about doing better for the sake of doing better.

At those times when you are just barely getting by, don't worry: there are enough developmental stages to go through that all parents get their turn at being good and not-so-good. Each developmental stage requires different traits, skills and personalities in the parent to make it go smoothly. You will bring your personal strengths and weaknesses to parenting, and you need to see these for what they are and deal with them head on. From either a position of ease or one of struggle, aiming for better will give you a framework to stimulate realistic ideas about how and when to stretch your abilities as a parent. Plan ahead.

Better is just in front of you at every developmental stage you'll face with your children. Better will always bring you to okay, but in those moments when you achieve great, go ahead and enjoy it!

Better is also about allowing yourself to make mistakes. Mistakes are the growing pains of parenting and you'll be a lot more prepared to look at your parenting (through reading this book or any other exercise) if you get comfortable with the idea of mistakes. Every so often, when all the stars and the moon are lined up in just the right order, things are right on with what gets said or done in parenting. However, most of the time efforts both succeed and fail; the trick is to make as many mistakes as necessary to rule out what doesn't work—as quickly as possible!

Keep the mistakes in mind, be okay with having made them, try not to repeat the same ones and keep the show on the road.

Aim for better—it feels great.

Chapter Three

Modeling

Modeling behaviors and attitudes for your children is another key to success in parenting, but this concept extends far beyond the idea of just "being a good role model." Modeling is an entire parenting strategy that involves identifying and choosing appropriate roles that enable you to parent effectively and to avoid pitfalls and scenarios where you will become stuck or even ineffectual. Modeling appropriate behaviors is a great start; using the idea that you can select from a huge variety of unique roles in your parenting is where it goes from a good idea to an important key for success.

As a parent, you already play a variety of roles. In fact, many of these roles can become a way you define yourself or are defined by your family. For example, many working parents refer to their perceived role as "provider," and stay-at-home parents frequently struggle with being perceived as "the maid, the gardener or the chauffeur." In order to use modeling as a strategy in improving your parenting, it is important to be conscious of the roles you play and of the language you use to define those roles. Doing this helps to prepare you for new modeling strategies that will offer better and more effective roles for you to adopt, as well as ways of changing any roles in which you have been miscast.

Of course, some roles work better than others. This section will stress the roles that help you navigate through the more difficult times, and the roles that bring more joy to your parenting. Once you've discovered a role that works for you and your children, add it to your repertoire! Then you can use it any time you like to make it easier for you to face the challenges of parenting. Building a repertoire of roles that work is a great goal for every parent, and having a menu of roles to choose from may be all you need to get past long-standing issues and start heading in a brand new direction. You'll find the roles of teacher, guidance counselor and coach suggested throughout this section, and you'll be encouraged to integrate them into your overall parenting strategy.

In this chapter you'll also find out about the roles you *don't* want to choose as you move through the parenting journey. Don't be shy—trade in what is no longer working, and add some new ideas that are more successful for you and your children!

Common Parenting Roles

**REST AREA
1 MILE**

Answering service	Manager
Attention giver	Married single parent
Banker	Mentor
Boss	Nurse
Butler	Party planner
Camp counselor	Problem solver
Coach	Provider
Concierge	Psychiatrist
Continual nag	Referee
Cook	Salesperson
Delegator	Short-order cook
Dishwasher	Spender
Eternal optimist	Super dad

Fashion consultant	Super mom
Guidance counselor	Sympathetic listener
Judge and jury	Taxi driver
Laundry worker	Teacher
Lifeguard/Rescuer	Timekeeper
Maid	Tutor
Maintenance service	Wake-up service

A quick review of this list may already have you thinking about the roles you play in your parenting. All parents have effectual and ineffectual roles in their repertoires, and all are capable of editing those roles in order to get to a better place in their relationship with their children. Some roles also fit certain situations better than others. For instance, parents of newborns might play the role of Nurse, whereas parents of healthy teenagers may want to be cautious with that one. Some roles need to go ASAP, and the less you play them the better you'll feel. Don't worry—the household will keep running. Go ahead—get rid of the Cook, Taxi Driver, Laundry Worker and Dishwasher, and replace them with a teacher and a coach; your kids will thank you in the end.

**REST AREA
1 MILE**

Don't forget that making mistakes in the roles you choose is part of the process. The faster you realize you have a habit of playing the Continual Nag, the Boss or the Laundry Worker, the faster you'll look for new, more effective roles.

You may discover that you are stuck in a role and unable to escape, no matter how hard you try. For example, you could find yourself in the role of private secretary to one or all of your children, and have difficulty imagining life in this family without you playing this role. You may even invent arguments that support your work as the family's private secretary. If you didn't keep track of everything, no one would get anywhere on time, know where they were supposed to be next, or show up for appointments and obligations—right?! At some point in the history of the family, likely when the children were much younger, this was both a healthy and an active role that added great value. In fact, being good at it then is something you still can be proud of to this day.

But now, ask yourself if this role is working with your four-teen-year-old (who manages to make numerous plans for the weekend but always misses the music lesson). Roles can outlive their usefulness but still remain entrenched in a family's daily life. And playing those roles can become quite frustrating. You, like many busy parents, may not have stopped to consider what roles you fill most often, or how to change them to suit the present needs of yourself and your family, but this simple recognition and shift can help keep things moving smoothly for years. Now is the time to incorporate a great new role that better suits your growing and changing family.

Consider these strategies in order to create positive change:

1. Think about whether playing a role you don't like is keeping other family members from developing, learning, growing or looking after themselves. A role you don't like might be one you play too often or have played for too long a period in your child's de-velopment. The chores and responsibilities that go with that role may be a positive force (encouraging self-esteem and community within the family) when in the hands of someone new!

2. Tell your family that you will no longer perform this role in the family. Don't do this because you are angry, but because you want to expend your energy on the roles you choose.

3. If you think it's the kind of role that "somebody's *gotta* do," share the responsibility with other adults, co-parents and people involved in your children's lives.

4. Notice when you are playing the role, then simply stop playing it. This isn't about making a fuss and letting everyone know; this is about being quiet and insightful and changing your attitude *and then* your behavior. Take up the challenge of "not doing." If you take a moment to *not* behave in these known (and expected) roles, the repetitive, age-old response will pass you by and something new and unknown will occur instead. Doing nothing for a moment or two often turns out to be the best action you can take.

You will also discover some roles you are really good at that perfectly suit your parenting style and your family. Entertain the possibility of expanding these roles. See what comes of playing a role consciously at times of crisis or just on a daily basis. The roles that work for you and the family need to stay on the menu!

There are three roles that almost always work for parents. These roles come fully equipped with time-tested parenting tools that help build better relationships, and keep the family environment safe and fun. They are the teacher, the guidance counselor and the coach.

Teacher

One of the most common problems faced by parents is that of encouraging their child to take part in the many lessons life has to offer, while keeping them safe. At some point all parents will find themselves teaching: teaching to color, to brush teeth, to cook . . . the list goes on and on. When the teaching goes well and the teeth are brushed, this feels good for parents and their children. However, in parenting this is only the very beginning of the usefulness of the role of teacher.

Teaching includes preparing your child for the many life lessons they will face that are outside of parental control. In these cases, it is often the parent's impulse to attempt to shelter the child from failures, to rescue, or to redirect the child in another, safer direction. It is difficult to allow children to learn through taking risks and experiencing on their own. Ultimately, parents in the role of teacher will be teaching their children how to deal with success *and* how to deal with failure as the journey progresses.

> **REST AREA 1 MILE**
>
> Teaching is about preparing your child for life lessons, but it is not about crime and punishment. The role of teacher is always a viable replacement for that of controller, boss, enforcer or dictator.

Parents tend to more easily adopt the role of teacher when they see their children heading for success; after all, their child's independent behavior is likely going to be reinforced in the lesson learned. In situations where there is a possible lesson to be learned through failure, parents find it much more difficult to think and act using the role of teacher. In these situations, one great trick is to focus on providing a safe place for your child to return to, where the parent as teacher can reinforce the lesson learned and help the child see the value it holds for them in decisions and actions.

At times life is like a science experiment, and children need to make their own observations, draw their own conclusions and decide on their own recommendations. Of course, anything that is life threatening is outside of the teaching model, but all else is a possible lesson in life. Effective teaching is measured not just by your child's ability to win and succeed, but also by how well they have learned to identify with the feelings of others and by their ability to balance pride with humility.

Let's say you offer your child a ride to school. The truth is that she could just as easily walk, but it will also be convenient for you to give her a ride. It all starts off innocently and with good intentions on your behalf. Needless to say, you have to leave at a specific time and this is not negotiable.

On the first day your child is not ready to go on time. This is one of those moments where you want to "teach" (read: lecture) your child about respect and co-operation, but with only half a cup of coffee in you, you'd prefer to just get out the door and off to work. On the way to school you find yourself saying how you can't be late and how sorry you are that you offered.

If in this situation you were to adopt the true role of teacher you could say to yourself, "This is a good time to teach a lesson about punctuality and the importance of being on time for work." So, instead of the usual nagging coming to mind, you simply say, "Sorry you weren't ready on time, I can't be late. Let's try again tomorrow." In spite of your child's promises that she'll just be a minute, etc., you leave. You are the teacher, and this is a lesson. When your child says, "I can't believe you left without me," you now have the option of saying, "This is about you not being ready; not about me leaving without you. Let's try again tomorrow. Remember, I have to be out of here right on time."

> The first lesson your child learns is:
> If I want a ride, I have to be ready on time.

> The second (and larger) lesson is:
> Work is important, and getting to work on time is important.

You'll begin to hear yourself saying things like "'Bye, Sweetie! Have a great day. Sorry I can't wait to give you a ride. Work is important and I can't be late! Love ya!" Then you leave. She learns a lesson (maybe for the tenth time) and you have exited as the teacher. No lectures, no nagging, no being late for work.

Teaching moves you away from viewing things in terms of punishment and from winning or losing, and consequently you avoid adopting the roles of warden, dictator and boss.

In teaching, you don't yell and punish, you teach! Lousy teachers yell and scream. Good teachers assist with the learning and have a sense of logical consequences. Take, for instance, the statement "You're late for the ride on days when I need to be on time, and so you walk—I don't wait." It describes the lesson, and the logical nature of the consequences clearly. The situation is then rooted in logic and not worth fighting about; it will just be another lesson worth learning along the way.

Keep in mind that the family is a place of safety and security, and as such it is the perfect spot for you to provide lessons for your children that will help them in the future. No, you don't have to be a real teacher, but at times it will help if you can act like one. Set your sights on practicing parenting through teaching until it becomes second nature—you'll avoid a lot of regrettable situations!

Guidance counselor

To model the guidance counselor you'll need to know what responsibilities these professionals have, and what tasks they perform. Broadly defined, guidance counselors listen, encourage and help kids come to their own solutions. They rarely tell kids what to do, but they do offer alternatives and choices. They want children to develop the skills to problem-solve academic, social or interpersonal issues, and not to just do what they are told.

Here's an illustration of when and where modeling the guidance counselor in your parenting can be helpful:

> Your son comes home fairly early from school and you say, "Hey, you're home early!" After a brief pause you hear your son say, "No one likes me. Today everyone went to play basketball and I wasn't invited. Life sucks."

You have lots of responses and things you'd like to say, but when the situation calls for listening skills to be put in place, it is generally time to play the role of the guidance counselor. The idea here is to listen, to offer alternatives and choices, and to encourage: the things the guidance counselor would be more likely to do than the parent. The parent is apt to jump into the role of protector, rescuing from hurt; or the role of friend, falling into the trap of distracting their child from feeling hurt by offering to play basketball with them; or, the role of problem-solver who offers a million suggestions as to what the child should do now. As a parent, the impulse is to jump to your child's defense, hoping to make things less painful. But let's take a look at what happens when the listening skills of the guidance counselor take over.

> "Wow, you must be pretty down about this. What do you think you'll do?"

The hard part here is to stop yourself from saying things like "Maybe you should . . ." and "Isn't so and so always calling?" and "How is so and so? Maybe they're available . . ."and "Maybe we should build a net at our house . . . " Edit all of this out of your conversation.

Listen. Encourage. Empathize. Support. *Guide* the lesson of life in this case; don't *teach* it. If you're lucky, your child may ask you what you think they should do, but don't be fooled at this point. Encourage them to come up with their own solutions. They'll find out you're there, you're listening and providing support, and that they are free to take advantage of the safety of this. They will also learn that they are not required to get caught up in the rights and wrongs of how they feel, which helps to keep communication open.

Using the role of guidance counselor allows both you and your children to see that in tough or emotional situations (both big and small) open communication is possible. You will grow stronger in your listening skills and your children will speak more freely as a result of really feeling listened to and heard.

The role of guidance counselor is particularly useful in that it encourages parents to participate in their children's lives in ways that respect the child's ability to solve and resolve issues. If used in the early stages of the journey, it can establish a style of communication that will become very valuable in parenting teens through some of the roadblocks they face in adolescence. If it is new to your repertoire of parenting roles, there's no time like the present to begin working at this one!

Coach

We all know what great coaches are and what great coaches do: challenge, encourage personal bests, provide words of wisdom, act as the calm and cool voice of reason and authority, and always make their point clearly. We also know that great coaches are effective from the sidelines and rarely ever wind up in the game itself. The role of coach is a valuable addition to any parenting repertoire.

Coaches acknowledge that the children are in the game, and that they themselves are on the sidelines. A great coach will be directing and suggesting, but is not invited onto the field, into the ring or onto the ice. For example, if your little one has friends over and they are leaving one child out, your first impulse may be to get involved in the activities or change the game they are playing. You *could* join them at this level, but consider the possibility of coaching: you can achieve exactly what you are hoping to by suggesting, commenting, reviewing the rules of the day and stepping out to see if the players can move to a better game strategy.

A good coach likes to see team players, everyone included in the win or the loss, and a sense of fair play—just what a good parent would like to see. The coach doesn't lecture, humiliate or single players out, and always focuses on the group, encourages positive team behavior and reinforces gains made toward common goals and objectives.

For many parents, the typical coach's post-game follow-up—the review of all the great things about the game and the players that day—is often missing. In the situation described above, the parent who has helped the little ones to include everyone in their play and focus on the team could easily and effectively conclude the playtime with a few encouraging words, reminding the children of the lesson learned by encouraging them to feel great about their positive role within the team.

Consider inserting the word coach into some of the parenting situations and dilemmas that you struggle with, and see if you can discover a unique and effective way to change your parenting. For example, consider the notion of the homework coach.

The Homework Coach

Homework is often a touchy subject for both parents and kids: "helping" children with their homework too often swings between actually doing the assignment for them and fighting continuously while trying to get them to do it themselves—to the point where the homework rarely ever gets done without a battle. Applying the strategies of effective sports coaching to homework can help parents avoid some of these pitfalls.

Looking to the coach as a model, there are certain constants already in place. The sports coach never plays the actual game, never wears the equipment, stays off the field or the rink, and says to the players: "You have to go out there and make this happen—I'm just the coach—you guys are in charge of the game."

In the same way that the sports coach is always on the sidelines and is never suited up for the game, the homework coach needs to make sure the "players" have all the equipment they need for the play—the homework coach never suits up for the game by holding the eraser and erasing, finding the pen and doing the writing, grabbing the calculator and getting the answer, finding the notebook and making the notes, or buying the crayons and helping to make the title page for the project.

What the coach does do is set up the plays and devise strategies for player success. Coaching is a fine balance between hands on and hands off, with the focus on the goal of the game. This means showing ways to do homework ("Let's do this at the desk"), setting up the plays that work ("Homework before TV"), and being available to assess and encourage the next move ("Gee, the home run here would be if you colored in all the letters").

The key in coaching is to resist jumping out onto the field or over the boards onto the ice and to let the players play their best game. In this way the coach plays a role in the overall success of the players, but is still able to congratulate the players on their performance and to assess failures in ways that ensure everyone knows who was responsible. Being a homework coach is a great idea, especially since there's already a teacher in the picture!

The homework coach, the bedtime coach, the household chores coach—all possibilities for great parenting from the sidelines. Remember that as the bedtime coach you don't hold the toothbrush and lay out the pajamas—you set up the game by demonstrating, running a few practices and having the players put things in place. The household chores coach can follow the same guidelines with how to toss the recycling and how to get those dishes to the sink. The players need to be busy, the coach is a sideline position.

Finding Greatness in Role Models

Everyone knows people who are good at the roles they play with children and who make excellent role models for those around them. The first step toward adopting these qualities is to reflect on who those people are and what exactly they are doing that makes them great. Take a good look around—you may have seen them at the rink, the school, the daycare, in your own past, or right there at the kitchen table.

When thinking about modeling your actions after someone you know, you can approach the process in two phases. Phase I is "Spotting Greatness." Phase II is "Applying Greatness."

Phase I: Spotting Greatness

Spotting Greatness is *more difficult* than it might appear at first glance. In the busy lives of today's parents, this kind of greatness is taken for granted more than anything else. Parents say things like "Oh, she's a great teacher—she really loves teaching," or "Wow, you were lucky to get such a great coach." More often than not, you will find that the great person right there in front of you is a mentor you could emulate in parenting, someone who can help you identify the specific qualities you are hoping to include in your overall parenting repertoire.

**REST AREA
1 MILE**

In the search for greatness, ask yourself:

Who are the great teachers I have known in my life, or encountered in my children's lives?

Who are the coaches that have brought greatness to my child's life?

Who are the individuals who have guided my children or a family member through open communication and helping?

What made them great?

The process of spotting greatness can help you discover teachers, guidance professionals and coaches, not just in your children's lives, but also in your own. Remembering and learning from the great individuals of your own childhood can also be a rewarding search. You can then broaden your search to include summer counselors, babysitters, older siblings, clergy and other religious persons, and many more. Be sure to do a 360-degree search when looking around yourself, your child and your family.

The search for greatness in your life will take place in every part of it, but the best chances for success are usually surprisingly close to home. Generally, people have had only a few mentors. Many say they have had only one or two in their lifetime, and most of those turn out to have been great coaches, teachers and guidance counselors.

And of course, the great parents you know are the ultimate in role models.

If you are lucky, you may find some parents who can take you the extra step, showing you how greatness can be applied on the parenting journey. The work they have already done in incorporating great teaching, guiding and coaching shines through, so you can see it all in its successfully synthesized form. There is nothing like a great parent close by who can act as mentor and can show you greatness in its applied state!

Phase II: Applying Greatness

Phase II is the process of applying the greatness you have actively discovered. Generally, this is much easier than the search, and it feels wonderful! The more you can apply what you have learned from your role models, the easier the whole parenting process becomes. To apply the skills you see around you, you'll have to first identify the things that are great about them.

For example, you may notice that a teacher is great because even in the worst of times she never overreacts, but you know that the inner workings of that teacher are those of a patient and sincere individual committed to working with children in ways that encourage them. The teacher likely avoids addressing inappropriate or unwanted negative behaviors that disrupt the wonderful things accomplished in the classroom—and does this as a result of her own commitment. The teacher sees the positive and always comments on it in ways that commend the child. This is the deeper level of understanding that you are reaching for as you begin the process of applying greatness.

You may think of the coach who never stops trying to help from the sidelines, or the coach who is adored because he believes in making the game about fun, and not about winning. But you'll also need to consider what is at the core of such individuals before you can really apply their skills and positive attributes in your own parenting. This next step is about recognizing other people's strength of conviction.

If you completed Phase I successfully and spotted examples of greatness that you would like to follow, it will help if you look at a particular area in your parenting when applying the new role. Use it to assist with common dilemmas, or to figure out and fix problem areas you may be facing. Let's use bedtimes as an example.

A New Approach to Bedtimes

Many parents report this as a time when they frequently find themselves and their children in the midst of unnecessary conflict. Parents often feel that they are not being listened to and they can become quite punitive, even after starting out with the best of intentions. Plan ahead! Ask yourself:

> If I use the role of teacher as a model in my parenting (based on a great teacher I have identified), how would bedtime start to look at my house?

> If I use the role of guidance counselor as a model in my parenting (based on a great guidance counselor I have identified), how would bedtime start to look at my house?

> If I use the role of coach as a model in my parenting (based on a great coach I have identified), how would bedtime look at my house?

> If I use the role of a parent that I know and wish I could be more like, how would bedtime look at my house?

Remember, this isn't about being perfect, only better. Better means less yelling, less conflict, better routines, better hygiene, further independence and easier communication. Perfect bedtimes—they're a moving target! Don't assume that even the great models you chose to follow in orchestrating your children's bedtimes are perfect; instead, try thinking about those models and what they might or might not do in your situation. Use this as inspiration to change your behavior and attitudes when putting the kids to bed.

The parent as coach encourages from the sidelines and doesn't fight about routines like brushing teeth and lights out, but celebrates success; the parent as teacher helps the child see the logic and consequences of routines and encourages the lesson of lights out on time; and the guidance counselor takes a moment to listen to the concerns of the child at lights out and helps the child find alternatives to begin to solve their own dilemma.

A man named Gerry heard me speak on this topic and asked to discuss his own parenting situation with me privately. The father of three school-age children, he was frustrated with the rut he was in, always sounding and behaving the same way with little or no sense of accomplishment in his parenting. Initially I asked Gerry to list five things he was good at, to begin the helping process from a position of strength. Once this was in place, Gerry was ready to proceed.

Gerry followed some steps that can be helpful in using role modeling in your own parenting. Here they are, in general terms.

Step 1: Identify the moments in your own parenting that are not working well for you and your children.

Step 2: Identify the roles you are playing at those moments (see list on pages 18–19).

Step 3: Choose the roles you would like to stop playing in order to move toward using teacher, coach and guidance counselor to replace them.

Step 4: Identify coaches, teachers and guidance counselors you think are great or who demonstrate greatness (including what you believe are their positive attributes) for you to use as the model.

Step 5: Decide which of the more desirable roles of parent as teacher, parent as coach or parent as guidance counselor would be easiest for you to adopt at any particular moment.

Step 6: Consider parenting from the role you think you may do best at as a starting point.

Step 7: Assess the successes and failures you experience using that role, and introduce other roles as you go along in your parenting.

Step 8: Fine-tune the art of using roles in your parenting and continuously improve on the skills needed to play each of these roles.

Step 9: Feel great and become a role model to others!

For Gerry, the idea that he could adopt a role, or what he called "a position," in his parenting was attractive because he felt he was being caught repeatedly in the same arguments and interactions with his children; he was lecturing them and becoming frustrated and, as a result, repeating himself "over and over again."

Gerry was motivated after the presentation he attended, so getting through the first three steps was easy. First, we made an effort to see what roles in his parenting he wanted to get rid of, and he came up with "lecturer," "boss" and "nag."

> *Joe:* Okay, so we know what roles you *don't* want to be playing. Let's look forward to replacing those with roles that are going to work. You said that in the search for role models you came up with the priest who helped guide youth when you were a child, your kid's swim teacher who made the job fun but got things accomplished, and your old hockey coach. Now the question is: can you decide which of these models will work best for you? You'll need all of them as models to work from, but which role do you think is your primary role—the role you can most easily slide into on a tough day of parenting?

> *Gerry:* I think I parent best from a coaching perspective. It's the role I'm most comfortable with.

For Gerry, this is the place to begin building. Starting with the role Gerry feels most comfortable in (coach) will allow him to have a positive experience in spotting and applying greatness. From here he can start to build the skills he needs to do this for the roles of teacher and guidance counselor. Soon Gerry will be able to identify times when he is playing roles he doesn't really want to play, and then be able to stop himself.

> *Joe:* So, let's start with coaching about half the time, and when things get easier you'll explore being the teacher and the guidance counselor. There are lots of other roles you will test out and work into your repertoire, but this is a great place to begin. We'll try and switch to using teacher and guidance counselor more and more often, until all three roles are easily available for you to adopt and you can pick and choose according to the situation. Let's see this as getting good at using roles in parenting and starting the learning from a position of strength. So, you're the coach and . . .

During our discussions, Gerry will explore most of the roles listed in this book. I call this "roll a role," because sometimes it is a kind of gamble, a roll of the dice, as you are figuring out and practicing which roles work. If you are thinking in terms of better, better means having all these roles in mind and knowing which ones to choose and how to apply them in your parenting.

Take a few minutes to try this on your own or with a friend or co-parent. The nine steps Gerry used can work for you, too. In the early stages it is important to test and retest and to assess how things are working for you and your children. Once you have started to sharpen this skill, you can move toward integrating roles that are less familiar to you—they will stretch your abilities as a parent.

Role modeling and choosing a role is about what you choose and about what you *decide not to choose* as you and your children continue on the long parenting journey. Teacher, coach and guidance counselor will always come in handy, but don't forget to look for other useful roles along the way.

Chapter Four

Parent in Alliance, Not in Opposition

We all have a sense of what opposition looks and sounds like. No one likes it.

It's about being at opposite ends of the spectrum, fighting against one another for territory and ending up with a winner and a loser. In parenting, oppositional thinking is unpleasant and unproductive for all parties. Now consider this: the opposite of opposition is alliance. Parenting in alliance means moving through all the experiences of parenting in a way that establishes the fact that you and your child are *in this together*.

When one person in a relationship becomes oppositional, it is easy to respond in the same way. This doesn't help much.

REST AREA 1 MILE

"Why aren't you talking to me?"
"I don't know, because you aren't talking to me!"

For the most part, parenting in alliance is most challenging during the second and third years ("terrible twos" into "troubling threes"), the sixth year ("you're not the boss of me!"), and, well, let's call it adolescence and leave out the brackets to describe it.

Factored into this equation is how oppositional you and/or your co-parent are individually, and the effect this has on your children. Adults who "can be stubborn," or who "have a one-track mind," or who "need to be right," can find themselves parenting in opposition far too often. To help you move toward better, the following section offers some strategies for parenting in alliance.

A question for you: *When disciplining children, is the goal to get them into trouble, or to help them get out of trouble?*

There is a big difference between the two ideas. Parenting in alliance means helping children get out of trouble as often as possible. (After all, they seem to get into enough trouble on their own!)

If you send the message "you're in trouble," in all likelihood you are about to engage in opposition. If you can replace it with the message "you're already in trouble, so how can I help you get out of it and not get into it again?" you will be able to create and strengthen the alliance in your parent–child relationship.

Parenting in alliance supports the idea that your children will come to you when they are in trouble, and that you will be seen as part of their solution. Yes, you can be a problem to them, too. But, if you want your children to discuss the really big stuff with you, you'll need to firmly implant the idea that your parenting is focused on helping them from a position of alliance.

The earlier this idea is put in place, the better your parenting will go. Start now! Identify areas where you are parenting in alliance, and then begin to build new ones. Get a fresh start in areas of constant opposition.

Approaching parenting with an alliance mindset will help you to quickly identify the common troublesome roles that you need to let go of as you turn to attaining your new goal—like boss, principal, detective, interrogator and dictator. These oppositional roles will never be helpful in the long run, and even in the short run they will sabotage your overall efforts to parent in alliance.

**REST AREA
1 MILE**

POWER STRUGGLES

An important aspect of parenting in alliance is recognizing and letting go of any behavior that suggests there is a power struggle between you and your children. You can parent through power struggles, but you will *be* a parent when you work in alliance. "Winning" with a two-year-old or a teen is never a reality: once they have you engaged in a power struggle, they have already won!

Be prepared for some hard work along the way. You might be entrenched in some oppositional roles and need to step back a few paces to avoid jumping into the scripted oppositional moments you are having with your children. You could be holding on to these oppositional responses or behaviors because they seem to work in the short term, or because they are what you experienced growing up. However, once you can see the positive impact of establishing and maintaining a relationship of alliance, the path will become more clear.

For example, let's look at a very common parenting role: the boss. Many of you have seen this role, experienced it in your childhood or are playing it right now in your parenting. Letting go of this role means you must stop *thinking it* as well as acting it out. The thoughts "I'm the boss around here . . . " and "As long as you live under this roof . . . " and "When *you* are paying the bills around here . . . " are all examples of parenting in opposition within the role of boss. They are hierarchical, and really don't work. In the short term you may see or hear what you want to in your children, but parenting is a long-term contract and relationship.

Something to think about:

There's a big difference in a family between saying "I'm the parent around here, and there are rules we all have to follow" and "As long as I'm the boss around here you'll do as I say." Not only is there a difference in what you are saying, but there's also a big difference in what a child hears. Whenever possible, your parenting should demonstrate a willingness to work with your children and the language you choose is one of the many variables that communicate this mindset to them.

In addition to language, you can use tone of voice, physical stance, facial expression and all other forms of body language to communicate a message of either alliance or opposition in your parenting.

The Parent in Opposition

You say: "As long as I'm the boss around here . . ." (finger pointing, red in the face, volume rising)

> They hear: My parent is on a power trip.
>
> This is a challenge.
>
> I must be the "employee" or underling in this setting.
>
> This family is run like the army.
>
> My parent is not a teacher or coach or guidance counselor.
>
> I may have to go on strike.

The Parent in Alliance

You say:"As long as I'm the parent around here . . . " (stern, direct glance, voice level and raised a bit)

They hear: My parent is in charge.

My parent is a teacher and a coach.

My parent is angry but not losing control.

I am a child learning about life, a member of this family team, being cared for.

To succeed with this, it is crucial to understand the importance and power of a clear, firm and *consistent* message that is presented from a position of alliance. Alliance is not a soft or ineffective version of opposition. Not being the boss does not mean that you are not in charge, or that the children now run the house. In fact, as you read on you will encounter parenting advice that is very much about being in charge. It is just that being in charge of ourselves comes first! Take charge of your roles, let go of being the boss so that your children can grow and learn alongside you, and keep the parent–child alliances strong.

Chapter Five

The Long View
See the Journey as a Long One

A great deal of parenting is about being in the moment. Children look to parents for immediate responses to their needs, especially early on in parenting when you are faced with the demands of hunger, tiredness and wet diapers. Mostly, we're busy with the events of the present, the NOW of it all.

This chapter will show you how to step back for a moment. The parenting journey begins long before you actually have children, and carries on far beyond whatever moment you find yourself in today. Taking a long view is an exceptionally simple and effective strategy for positively changing your perception of the present—almost instantaneously.

Start at the Beginning

As a small child, you probably played house or dolls, dreaming of having a little one and being a great dad or mom. As a teenager you might have planned where you'd live and how many children you would like to have. As a young man or woman, your life before parenting possibly included being a coach, a swim instructor, a summer counselor or a babysitter. And now, here you are: coaching, teaching swimming or babysitting your own children!

We have become so aware of this pre-parenting planning that many schools now offer Family Studies and Parenting courses for high school credits. Even the schools have been surprised at the number of students keen to sign up and learn. When I'm lucky enough to be invited to speak to a group of students at a high school, the questions "How many kids do you want to have?" and "What kind of a parent do you want to be?" are enough to get the discussion rolling. At these early stages in their adult lives, their projections, hopes and dreams are still closely connected to the families they are living in now. The daughter of the recent divorce wants kids but not marriage; the only child of the professional couple hopes to have twins so her children won't have to play alone too much.

Your early thoughts about children were also guided by how you were being parented. Instead of being surprised by the effects of these early understandings in the middle of parenting your own children, it is helpful to stop and search them out in your own time, and on your own terms. This will give you time to learn through insight, instead of just being reactive when unconscious or early-formed ideals come into play.

Here's an example:

> Susan's mother yelled all the time. Early in her life, in the middle of all of the noise, Susan went out on the porch and silently promised herself that when she had children, she wouldn't yell at them. She really meant it. As she was growing up she often reminded herself of her internal vow. One day, when Susan was a mother, she yelled at her children. She was deeply shocked: she felt she was a failure and bad parent, and someone who could not keep her promises or live by

her most important code of ethics. Then, in the midst of feeling overwhelmed, she realized that the way she was yelling at herself sounded familiar, too.

Susan started the parenting journey early. She brought all her experiences, projections and promises with her to the creation of her own family, unaware that some of the commitments she'd made were those of a child on a porch with no understanding beyond that of her own limited experience.

Susan needs to understand her early-formed parenting promise—in this case the promise to *never* yell—and then use this childhood decision to direct, not define, her parenting. In doing so she will encounter the fears and the hopes that motivated her original promise. She can then reflect upon those fears and hopes to better understand her current sense of conflict as a parent. This process allows parents to integrate new, applicable, *adult* goals that will ease the current tensions popping up as a result of unrealistic (and powerful) early promises to themselves.

The Long View for Two

Being a co-parent can both deepen the joy of parenting and make things more complicated. Co-parents have had different childhood experiences, and will have made individual parenting promises to their individual selves (including those who have made none at all!). Let's look at how one couple ran into unexpected trouble, and found their way through, using the Long View.

> Al and Debbie were incredibly willing to make things work in their family, and they actively created common ground in order to understand one another and provide a basis for teamwork as co-parents.

Al's family was loud: lots of yelling and lots of fear. Debbie came from a home with seven children—she was the youngest and the only girl.

As their first child moved into the toddler years, Debbie noticed that she was parenting more than she had been, and that Al had started to yell more often. She hadn't heard much yelling from Al up to this time, so she was surprised by it. At first she made jokes about it, reassuring Al that the little one's hearing was okay. Eventually Debbie asked Al not to yell, and there was sudden friction in their relationship. Al felt attacked by her criticism and told Debbie that she was too sensitive, and that he'd "say whatever he wanted in his own house." Finally, one night, as this conflict was being aired in front of their child, he found himself yelling again, this time at her. "Stop criticizing me in front of the kid!"

All the way from the planning through to the childbirth, it never struck Debbie or Al that there might be a parenting issue for them to resolve. Until conflict was in front of them, neither had broached the subject in the context of raising their own children.

It was time for Al and Debbie to think long term in their parenting. Like many couples, they became entrenched in an argument and needed a way out, a fresh look at the current conflict that would encourage insights (into the past) and optimism for the future. They needed to "think long."

To start the process, they agreed to take a moment to recall their respective families of origin, the styles of parenting they had each experienced and the early agreements or promises they had made to themselves as a result. They then examined how these combined experiences were helping shape their current parenting practices, and whether their early-formed concepts of parenting were proving useful or detrimental.

Thinking long encouraged Al and Debbie to see the ongoing effects of their current conflict, including possible outcomes for their children, which ranged from low self-esteem as a result of the detrimental impact of being yelled at to conflicts of loyalty arising from having to operate within their parents' divided relationship.

Self-Examination: The Family of Origin

Every individual, couple and co-parent can benefit from looking at the past and understanding how it influences their current parenting.

Your family of origin has shaped many pieces of your own parenting puzzle, giving an endless array of implicit and explicit messages about all aspects of family life. Included in these are the following:

1. What a parent's social life looks like

2. What boys do and what girls do

3. What to do when there is a problem with a child

4. Ideas about money, allowance and children working

5. Ideas about education

6. Ideas about food and eating

7. The importance of friends, friendship and company at your home

8. Ideas about daycare and childcare

9. Ideas about telling children the truth about unpleasant, real-life events

10. The appropriate roles of family friends in a family's life

11. The importance of volunteering and giving in the community

12. Ideas about chores for kids

13. Ideas about putting effort into the act of parenting (talking about it, taking courses)

You can start the self-examination with the favorite question "Where did I come from?"

Are you a biological child of two parents? Were you adopted? Were you raised by close relatives? Did you go to boarding school at an early age? Were you parented by professionals? Did you live in a church-sponsored orphanage? Did you live in a typical nuclear family? Did you come from a single-parent family? A step-family? Where did you come from?

The next question is "What was (and perhaps still is) my status in the family of origin?"

Where did you fit in the sibling group in your family? It is important to find the language to define yourself in the sibling group in order to identify a sense of the place you came from. Were you an only child? Do you see yourself as the middle child? Would it be important to identify yourself in gender terms such as "the first child and only son in a family of daughters?" A twin? The older twin? Have you spent your life as "the baby of thirteen kids?"

Once you begin to see how the context of your family of origin has influenced your view of the world, take a moment to reflect. You may find yourself thinking, "I like to get my own way in terms of how the children are disciplined" and suddenly realize "as the youngest growing up, it was easy to get my own way" or "as an only child there was only my way!"

Now you can begin to consider other variables in your definition of self, such as traumas and losses experienced in your family of origin, personal development issues (puberty, weight, height, etc.), personal successes and failures, and the roles that others (including extended family) played in shaping your early experiences.

Consider Simmie's discoveries as an illustration of how some factors from the past were at play in her parenting.

> Simmie was the eldest child of immigrant parents. She saw the world in very concrete and practical terms. Her parents spoke a foreign language (Russian) and she just assumed it was her job to do the speaking for them. At age twelve she had been in her new country for one year and already she was at the bank filling out mortgage papers for her parents. After school, she worked in the family's store and placed all the orders with the salespeople. Her younger siblings eventually went to school and also learned to speak English, but by then Simmie was the default helper/doer in the English-speaking world for her mom and dad.
>
> When Simmie became a mother, everyone marveled at how she was "so capable." She was able to do the parenting, work full-time, continue to be the one to help her parents out, and manage things in her volunteer job. But behind the scenes, Simmie was getting worn down by the challenges of a husband who left everything to her and two children who did nothing around the house. Being the "doer" in all areas of her life was coming to a head, especially in her relationships with her husband and her children.
>
> She resented the role she played and was acutely aware of how little the rest of the family did. Things she "just did naturally" were suddenly becoming job-like for her, and she struggled against the urge to complain and nag constantly. Simmie recognized that she needed to take the Long View for a period of time to see if she could navigate her way out of this position.

Taking the time to look back gave Simmie a chance to see the influences of her previous family experiences on her current life as a parent and as a wife. She was able to see that she had always helped and done for others as "the good daughter and sister." She also saw that those around her had reinforced and encouraged this role—for instance, others in the community were always commenting on what a helpful daughter she was to her parents.

She acknowledged that she had grown up too fast, and that this had allowed her the great feelings associated with being trusted and depended upon. Simmie was surprised to discover that some of her experiences in this role resulted in fun. For example, she used to write her own notes for school, and it was never a problem to get mom and dad to sign them because they had no idea what was written! Being the "doer" had included some positives, helping explain why she may have chosen the role of "the capable one."

Simmie used the strategy of thinking long to connect the dots of her past, her present dilemmas and her future directions. She recognized the parallels between her role as wife and mother and her role in the family she grew up in, and acknowledged that her husband and her children were relying on her in part because she encouraged their behavior.

Taking the Long View helped Simmie see what she was holding on to and *why* she was holding on to it, in spite of not liking where she was. Most parents will discover similar dichotomies when examining their most common parenting roles. Examples are all around: the "pleasant one" who is sick of not being taken seriously but likes the notion of being liked by everyone; or, the "busy bee" who speaks wistfully of quiet time, yet cannot face the fear of being alone.

Looking Back and Moving Forward

David's dad died suddenly when he was eleven years old. David often said that he and his mom grew up together: they looked after everything from dishes to finances as a team. David always talked about how hard his mom worked in order to give him a good and full life. When David married and had children, his wife, Carolyn, was a stay-at-home mom (he liked that phrase) and was—much like his own mother—devoted to the children in their minute-by-minute lives.

When their youngest was seven, Carolyn decided to return to the workforce on a contract that employed her four days per week. Shortly after this, David became overly concerned about the children, their well-being and the role their mother was now playing in their lives. Carolyn heard David's thoughts as criticism, and stood her ground as a working parent.

Eventually David had to confront his fears about the children's well-being. After all, it was clear that they were all doing well, and had adjusted to their mom's return to work. In order to understand what was influencing him today, David spent a lot of time thinking about his mother and how she was a model parent for him because he had always felt she was "there for him."

Initially, Carolyn made a point of reassuring David that she was available to the children if need be. This did not help calm him down. In one of their discussions Carolyn said, "Well, you're here, too. There are two of us." At that point things became quiet.

"What does that mean?" he asked.

Carolyn realized they were now in trouble. In all of the chatter about his mother being there and Carolyn not being there, they had never discussed his father's absence.

In a flash, Carolyn asked, "After your dad died, did you and your mom ever talk about him, his death, anything like that?" David answered, "No," and from there the tears began. Carolyn realized she had never seen David cry. Ever. She had never heard him talk about his dad, either. Strange that until that moment she had not realized that David's dad, his death, and how it changed his life (let alone how it shaped their marriage and the parenting of their own kids) had never been brought up by either of them. Somehow they had created a family that talked about and processed its own events, yet not the events that were central to one of its founding members.

Eventually the conversations became less painful. The judgments and criticisms David had been imposing on Carolyn were now tempered with understanding on both of their parts. As time went on, Carolyn went to a three-day-a-week contract—not because of David, but because she needed the time for herself! David started seeing how important he was in the children's lives, without fear of suddenly being removed, and began the road to telling his children about their grandfather and about his own childhood days. Carolyn and David were moving forward in a new way on their parenting journey, integrating the events of the distant and recent past into a new and positive approach to creating a healthy, happy family.

Thinking Long Means Looking Ahead, Too

Taking the Long View is also about gaining perspective by thinking long into the future. In fact, many of the stresses of parenting involve being locked in the pressing moments of the day without seeing a way out. In these cases, thinking long offers a perspective that can bring joy to some of the more difficult moments along the way.

Here's a classic example of thinking long to gain perspective:

> Alan is a very active dad. He has one son named Jeffery who is two years old and who used to be defined as "the bright one" and the "the active one," and is now defined as "the stubborn one" because he doesn't use the toilet. Alan is concerned that Jeffery may be "late" in his development.
>
> Alan's mother fueled this fire by saying, "In our day we had them using the toilet at a year." His father then added, "Mother, when we were in England, wasn't there a lad under a year who used the loo?" Needless to say, this really didn't help Alan. His son Jeffery, on the other hand, was in no rush at all.

There's no daycare policy, special date or other parameter being imposed on Alan's thinking. Alan is caught in the moment, and he is submerged in a system of comments and ideas that have turned toilet training into a big issue and a source of stress. Alan needs perspective, and he can get it by thinking long. In his journey, he needs to pull over to the side of the road and remind himself that this is a stop-over, and not a final destination.

When you have moments like this along the way, and all parents do, it would be great if you could remind yourself that parenting is a long journey and that whatever issue you are facing is likely just a stop-over. Pressure, especially parenting pressure, creates an innate desire to fix things IMMEDIATELY! In those moments when it is difficult to think long, remind yourself that there is a long road ahead, and plenty of time for lessons, building skills, and love. This simple reminder will relieve unnecessary pressure in parenting and make room for in-the-moment joy.

Thinking long gives you permission to relax and enjoy the moment. It doesn't mean you are ignoring problems or in denial. The goal to toilet train, or to help your kids pick a career, or whatever it is that is creating pressure, is still in place; releasing the pressure of "this must happen right now—this minute" offers the relief that might be badly needed. In fact, once the pressure is off, you'll often think more clearly and find solutions and alternatives that you could not see while the pressure was pushing you along. Working under pressure in parenting, as in other areas of life, won't necessarily bring you to your best outcomes.

Try to add thinking long to your repertoire of parenting skills. See it as a way to rescue yourself during intense moments.

Thinking Long Means You'll Get To It Eventually

Taking the Long View also means long-term planning. In parenting this is a big plus. Unlike in other areas of your life, this approach means sometimes you *can* put off until tomorrow what you could do today. As an expert on yourself, your children and your family, you can get better at this, too!

Here's an example of how long-term planning can help in those awful short-term struggles.

Sandra, like many moms, can't stand hearing her infant cry. The baby cries, she goes to the baby. It's as simple as that. Lots of people tell her, "You have to let the baby cry. Don't worry. The baby is fine." But the baby cries and Sandra goes to her. People say: "You'll spoil her." "The baby is running your life." "If you don't start bedtime routines now, you'll be in trouble." "Wait until she's in a big bed. Then you'll really have trouble at bedtime."

But the baby cries and Sandra goes to her. Sandra eventually loses interest in what others tell her. She has to do what she has to do to suit herself. She realizes she'll have to pick up the pieces later.

Sandra knows that she cannot stand that the baby is crying when she doesn't know why. Sandra tells herself,

When the baby can talk, I'll have to catch up with putting bedtime in place and getting her used to me not coming whenever she calls. I can't do that now; I'll have to do it at the next stop along the journey. When the baby can talk, I will put these things in place, not now. I have from now until she goes to college. I'll start reading about putting your toddler to bed so I can know enough to catch up with all the good things everyone is so afraid I'll miss. Now is now.

As Sandra's journey unfolds she develops a short-term plan and a long-term plan that fit together. Sandra is becoming a mother on the journey. She is also becoming an expert on herself. The advice offered to Sandra by others is neither good nor bad.

Sandra has let go of others' ideas as to how her family should look; she wants to do a great "Sandra job" at being a parent and making a family.

Seeing the journey as long is about perspective, but it is also about opportunity. Being a parent provides a variety of opportunities, especially the opportunity to do your best and to grow and change. In fact, many people like Alan and Sandra learn this in parenting and apply it in the rest of their lives. Parenting isn't only a challenge—it may even be good for you!

Chapter Six

Parenting on Three Words a Day
Love and Limits

In today's busy world, parenting can be overwhelming. What initially appeared to be a simple life-task called "having a few kids," is at times enough to bowl anyone over! The following strategy is designed to help alleviate the stress and strain of finding yourself in a quagmire of parenting, and to provide a framework that will guide and reinforce all the choices you make.

Just as the perplexed traveler finds comfort in a text like *Europe On Five Dollars a Day,* parenting travels can be simplified and navigated more easily with a guide mapped out by someone who has seen it all.

First Comes Love

There will never be enough written about this topic. Telling your children "I love you" is simple and workable. There are a million and one ways to do this, and it really works. How many ways do you have of expressing your love to your children? Verbally? In writing? By saying aloud all the variations of "I love you" from "I like you" to "I'm proud of you" to "I heard something nice about you" to "You must feel great," and so on? Make sure your message is heard! If you do this naturally, you're lucky. If you have to work at it, then work at it—and then you'll be lucky. Trust me, the more effort you put into this, the luckier you'll get. Clearly expressing love in uncomplicated ways sets the scene for loving with limits, the ultimate framework for effective and joyful parenting.

What does parenting look like without open expressions of love? The painful experiences of many fathers and sons who waited until the emergency and immediacy of deathbeds before they could find the courage to say "I love you" have taught us a lot about this. For these men, and maybe for you, a lot of time was wasted between people who loved each other. If you are not good at saying "I love you," now is the time to start doing something about that. Stop wasting time. Say it out loud. Practice if you have to. These three words will provide an unshakable base for the parenting structure; this foundation will deepen the good times and see you through the bad; it will lend strength and fairness to your discipline; and it will crank up the volume on your celebrations!

The I Love You "Cover-Up"

If you are busy supporting a parent who doesn't say I love you, just a word to the wise: stop it. Don't cover for a partner by saying "You know she loves you even if she doesn't say it." You are wasting your time "interpreting." Instead, pull over to the side of the road and let them tell each other. Stop. Stay there as long as it takes. You can be of immense help by encouraging communication between your loved ones. From the child's perspective, hearing that a parent loves them from anyone other than that parent is second-best. If they are here and able to tell the children themselves, let's get to it!

I love you is not the "soft approach" and it is not meant to mask conflict or to replace the need for discipline. In spite of the truth of this, some parents fear that by saying "I love you" they will lose control over their children, or send them a message that "anything goes." In fact, it is just the opposite. Telling your children you love them establishes why you are disciplining or guiding them at any given moment. The next section will expand on this notion with the introduction of limits and limit-setting.

Then Comes Limits*

It is important to begin with talking about love, but the real strength of parenting is the balance of love and limits, not either one on its own.

In setting limits for and with your children, you are challenged to help your children express themselves in healthy ways, within acceptable behaviors and attitudes. Also, setting limits for your children is an ongoing process: it should slowly and gradually turn into your children setting limits for themselves.

What kind of limits?

For preschoolers you may need to put limits on a range of behaviors. For some, the limits will be designed to discourage unacceptable behaviors such as hitting, kicking and biting; whereas for others limits will be created that encourage such behaviors as sharing and eating at the table. In all cases, the limits will depend on the parent presenting clear guidelines and consequences that remain consistent until the children can limit their own behavior.

For older children, setting limits may connect to more complex social behaviors; for instance, making fun of others or excluding others. With adolescents, setting limits will involve much more trust and negotiation, and cover an ever-broader scope as teenagers' lives grow to involve more and more of the world, underscoring the need for them to set healthy limits for themselves.

When it comes to setting limits, remember:

If they could do it themselves, they would. That's why you're here!

To set effective limits, you need to create an environment where children understand that you care about them. Love and Limits as a parenting strategy depends on this. In an atmosphere of anger, frustration or power struggles, limits and boundaries feel like punishment handed down from an authority figure. In an environment of love, children will interpret and respond to your limits as what they are: advice-giving, protection and caring.

★ *Special thanks to Joe Kronick of Camp White Pine, Haliburton, Ontario, for passing this along to me in its camping form early on in my career!*

"Negotiables" and "Non-Negotiables"

Define the limits you set as "negotiable" and "non-negotiable." Your children should not have the feeling that your word is *always* cast in stone, and they also need to know which words *are* carved in stone. By establishing that limits are either negotiable or non-negotiable, you encourage your children to learn some negotiation skills, and to know when they are wasting their time.

There should be few non-negotiables in your parenting, and lots of more flexible rules and boundaries that are appropriate to the age and stage of your child; keeping in mind that these are limits that will shift and change with their emotional, social and physical growth.

RE-NEGOTIATIONS

If you can't sleep because of something you have agreed to with your child, in all likelihood you have negotiated a non-negotiable. At this point you will need to re-think your position and return to the parent–child relationship to discuss the dilemma. Even though it is difficult to go back to your child and reset a more restrictive limit, if they know you set all limits out of love, time will heal the situation at hand and they will be able to see that the new and less palatable limit is set from the same love.

Remember this—take action from a place of love and caring—then go back to sleep!

If everything you say sounds like it can't be negotiated, children will eventually explode or rebel beyond what is normal or realistic to expect. "We'll do that later" has to sound and feel a lot different from "No playing on the road." Your children should react differently to each, feeling free to try their skills at negotiating what "later" could mean, and accepting that the message in "No playing on the road" is firm and consistent, said with love, and non-negotiable.

Often what is set in stone at one age or developmental stage will change at a future stage. In fact, every rule you create will eventually become negotiable, until your children become young adults and are in charge of setting their own limits and bearing the painful and pleasurable consequences of this. Let's take, for example, an eight-year-old who wants to play street hockey. There are a lot of variables to consider if this is a child who has never been allowed to play on the road. The parent skilled at working with love and limits will recognize this as a perfect time for the child to practice negotiating. Rather than getting stuck with yes or no, which limits both the child's growth and the parent's opportunity to see the child's increasing maturity and skills, you can say:

"You know I love you and worry, so you'll have to convince me of whether or not you are allowed to re-negotiate the rule we have had for so long."

At this point, the child will have to identify the concerns about playing on the road (have they heard a word you've said over the eight years?) and will have to identify what limits they are willing to put in place for themselves to make this work. Just saying "Aw, come on, mom" a hundred times until mom wears down will not be negotiation, and will not work. If you are lucky (some of parenting is about luck) the child may say,

"I promise I'll watch for cars and I'll come home before it gets dark."

Negotiations can then continue from there. For example, you might say:

"How about I come and watch the first time or two and you show me this. I won't say when it is time to go, you will!"

Or

"How about playing on the side street next to our busy street for starters, and we'll see how you do at getting home on time?"

The situation above can easily land at "no," or at "let's think about it," or at "yes." The important part is that what was non-negotiable is now up for negotiation and discussion! Negotiating with your children is also a good way to teach them negotiation skills. However, bedtime is still nine o'clock—only negotiate one limit at a time.

Interactions like these with your children begin to open up the lines of communication within the parent–child relationship. While the children are assuming greater responsibility, you can also see them demonstrating the improved listening skills necessary for future negotiations while building self-esteem and confidence in the process. Ultimately the positive spin-off for the parent is the increasing sense of comfort with the fragile process of gradually letting go—handing over the reins to children who are demonstrating to a certain extent that they are ready.

It is important for children to develop skills in negotiation in the safety of their own home and family. Parents face the more complex task of negotiating and teaching negotiation skills at the same time. Teaching the following will be helpful to your children regarding limits and negotiations:

1. Your children have the right to question and negotiate: this (within your home and family) is where they can build these skills in a safe way. Parents have the right to decide the limits set within negotiations—including the definition of what is non-negotiable.

2. These negotiations take place between people who love each other, and nothing will be outside of that base.

3. Don't waste too much time arguing the non-negotiables.

4. Successful negotiations will often revolve around your child's willingness to reassure you. You can teach them that, for example, a call home during the afternoon downtown, or a call to say good-night from the party, will be a very important part of their later negotiations.

5. One item at a time—too many items make all negotiations complex.

6. There must be a time-frame established for all negotiations. For example, you and the children agree that the decision about a Saturday trip with friends will be settled by the Friday before; if they need an answer *now,* then "no" will have to do.

7. One negotiation can lead into the next negotiation; as children uphold their end of one bargain, parents are reassured and the next negotiation is more likely to go well.

BEWARE THE GREAT NEGOTIATORS!

Children have to stick to what they say in negotiations and give you the feeling that the end has justified the means. Negotiation in healthy relationships is not a snow job or an exercise in pulling the wool over your eyes, and this needs to be established throughout the child's growing years.

Successful negotiations in the parent–child relationship rest on the same principles as those in all relationships: negotiate one item at a time, build trust before moving on to the bigger items, and don't make promises you can't keep.

Three Other Words

Love and Limits is a fantastic place to begin, but there may be three words of your own that can work for you in keeping it simple. (At a recent parenting presentation I suggested the audience come up with their own three words that characterized their ideal parent–child relationship. A man called out: "Three words? How about ASK YOUR MOTHER?!" Let's hope he's reading this book, too.) Regardless of what three words you select, the rule is to keep the parenting as simple as you can, both in your own mind and in your parenting and co-parenting decisions. Don't worry, no matter how simple you like to keep it, the journey of parenting will get complicated without your help. Three words for a complicated and overwhelming day: keep them handy.

Chapter Seven

Yes, No, Maybe

Like a traffic light's green, yellow and red, the three words Yes, No and Maybe are enough to keep a family out of most traffic jams. In fact, when used in the context of love and limits suggested in the previous chapter, these few words can take you to a whole new level of effective parenting for children of all ages and developmental stages.

REST AREA 1 MILE

Yes means: "It is 100% possible if up to me."

Maybe means: "It is a 50/50 chance."

No means "It is "100% not possible if up to me."

It is true that there is an art and science to saying all three words. Knowing when to say them and how to say them (and sticking to them!) can be trickier than you think. Sometimes you're in an artful parenting moment where your yes, no or maybe just rolls out of your mouth and makes perfect sense to you and the child. At other times, you realize that what you thought you said isn't necessarily what they heard.

Here are some helpful hints for successfully using Yes, No and Maybe.

No—The Word No One Likes to Say and No One Likes to Hear

Parenting requires saying no more frequently than most relationships. At times the burden of saying no and being seen as the mean mom or dad can be difficult for many adults. In addition to facing not being liked, saying no can lead to altercations with your children and the added necessity (often at the busiest of times) of teaching them how to cope with hearing and experiencing refusal.

Hearing no and coping with not always getting what they want is good for children. It helps to build the skills they will need for the world outside the family. When they hear their boss say no to a vacation, they'll know how to handle it because you have taught them the skill of hearing no in a loving and limit-setting environment. Though it may seem contradictory, saying no effectively is an important aspect of parenting in alliance rather than in opposition.

There often isn't an easy road when it comes to saying no, but these lessons will help make the process less painful.

Meaning "No" When You Say It

> Deanna is at the neighborhood drugstore. She is at the checkout waiting to pay. There's the candy, placed nicely in those little trays that let you see all of them. Her two-and-a-half-year-old is screaming, "I want

candy," over and over again. People are staring. It's half an hour before lunch, her child has just had juice, and they will be out of the store in thirty seconds. There is no reason to buy this candy and give it to her child, but Deanna feels caught.

No one wants to get stuck in this moment, but almost everyone does. You already know it is hard for Deanna to win. If she buys the candy, people see her as giving in and being "a soft touch," and her child will learn that a scene in public gets you what you want. If she doesn't buy the candy, her child will continue screaming and others may judge Deanna's parenting based on her child's behavior. You've been there. What to do?

Laying down a consistent pattern with regard to saying no is a huge help in moments such as this one. Through repetition, children learn to manage their disappointments and to either identify ways they can get to yes, or to recognize when they are wasting their time and yours.

In the above situation, Deanna can start by using what she has learned so far, thinking long to get some perspective and then choosing a role to help her implement a firm and loving way of saying no to her child.

For example, Deanna can tell herself:

This will pass.

This is a long journey. This is minor. It's not even a stop-over at the side of the road.

This behavior is normal for this age. Every parent here who is a parent knows what this is like.

I can do this.

I have nothing to prove. This is just one moment of my parenting.

If I play the role of teacher, what am I teaching by giving in?

Do I want to teach that bad behavior gets you what you want?

If I play the role of coach how can I encourage my child from the sidelines to re-approach the situation and stay calm?

Take pride in not losing your cool and in sticking to your good judgment. This is good for the child, and it is also good for the parent in terms of feeling confident in their parenting and being prepared for the big moments in parenting that will really require the big NOs. Parents who can say no are proud of themselves.

Strategies for Tantrums

Many parents find that they are great at saying no until their child throws a tantrum, when all planning seems to fly out the window. There are some specific strategies you can add to thinking long, choosing a role and aiming for better. In the case of a tantrum, try the following suggestions:

- Don't take the tantrum personally. This situation happens to all parents at the checkout counter.

- Don't engage in the behavior. Don't look your child in the eye or make any engaging gestures. Try to maintain the position of observer.

- Comment on the behavior. ("Wow, you need to work on mommy/daddy saying "no." or "You don't like no.")

- Remember why you are in the drugstore (did you come in to get shampoo or to make a scene?) and stick to your purpose. Don't let preschoolers change the agenda because they haven't yet learned to control their wishes and wants.

- Say, "this is unacceptable" as a way of explaining, not disciplining. Try to get your child out of trouble, not in trouble. Use this time to teach your child to discuss when there is something that he or she wants.

- Identify yourself in one of your roles and see what that means right there at the checkout counter.

- Don't abandon your task or punish your child because he or she wants candy. All kids want candy. It's not a punishable offense.

- Let it go, for you and for them. Don't allow an event like this to spoil a day or evening. It is a short moment on the long journey; don't make it any longer or larger than it has to be. Make the good stuff last longer.

- Don't trade this problem for another by saying things like "I'll buy it for you now, but you can't eat it until later." Say no, take your lumps, and move on to the next part of your day.

- Remember that you have to manage your behavior before you can teach your children to manage theirs.

Shaleen's preschooler, who is tired, whining and has missed his nap, spies a toy he wants. Shaleen sees the situation coming and knows she is about to say no to an overtired boy at the end of a long day. People are watching. Shaleen thinks to herself, "Think long, and be clear, firm and consistent."

Jarod: I want dolly!

Shaleen: You can't have dolly . . . we have a dolly at home.

Jarod: I want dolly!

Shaleen: Mommy said no.

Jarod: (kicking and in full tantrum mode): I want dolly! DOLLY!!!

Shaleen: No.

Shaleen pays for her purchase, gets Jarod out of the store, and he falls asleep the instant she buckles him into the carseat.

Good for Shaleen. There's no dolly and that's it. Just tears and noise.

Like many of us, Shaleen optimistically begins with the phrase "we have a dolly at home," that *implies* no. Although there is adult logic to this, it rarely works. To children, especially tired ones aiming for yes, this sounds like a phrase open to negotiation. She may avoid using no at the first request for dolly because she is hoping to avoid the tantrum, rather than having to use more energy to teach, mentor and guide her son through this. Simple is good. Saying no at the start is simple. Teaching children to be good at dealing with no is important, and her little one is in the early stages of learning.

Other Ways to Say No

Over time you'll become bored with just no, so consider expanding your skill set. Here's a summary of ways to say no that I hope will amuse and encourage you. Use these to experiment, build a repertoire and even keep the children entertained! Have a look at these and invent some of your own, keeping in mind that the more humorous, sarcastic and non-verbal versions may be for special moments and audiences, and not the way to teach no in the early stages.

The definitive no: "N.O."

The apologetic no: "Uh-uh, sorry."

Funny-sentence no: "No can do."

The paradoxical no: "Yeah, right."

The let-you-down-easy no: "Don't see that happening, pal"

The cool and hip no: "Wake up, you're hallucinating!"

The "dumb" no: "Nope."

The other-language no: "Nee-yet" (Russian) "Nada" (Spanish for "nothing" but often close enough in the right context.)

The sarcastic no: "Which part of NO don't you understand?"

The clarifying no: "This *no* will not turn into a *yes*."

The fed-up no: "No means no."

With older children who are more apt to try to negotiate, you can use a "three-strike system." Here's a moment on Perry's parenting journey that we can use to demonstrate.

STRIKE ONE
"Dad, can I go to the mall?"
"*No.*" (The definitive no. You're sure about this one.)

STRIKE TWO
"Please, please, everyone is going!"
"*Yeah, right.*" (The paradoxical no—works for the younger teen. A bit of respectful playfulness on dad's part; they both knew this second attempt was going to come up and Perry uses humor to try to get around it.)

STRIKE THREE

"This isn't fair. Everyone is going. You baby me. This is stupid. I'll have no friends just like you and mom because I never go out!"

"Boy, you are really bad with 'no.' You need to work on this."

When Perry and his daughter Rachel hit strike three the exchange is over. Perry is ending it, not the child. Perry is being the best father he can be, and is saying no. He's not lecturing, and most important, he's not engaging or escalating. He understands her wishes and her dilemma, and is telling his child that there is a boundary and that she needs to work harder at understanding and accepting no for an answer. It's great parenting!

One successful experience with no won't mean your children will accept them all gracefully, but each success is an important building block that enables you to parent within the limits that sit comfortably with you.

Body Language

Think of the gestures for no (and for yes and maybe) as part of the coaching of parenting. A coach uses and teaches gestures that allow players to communicate on the field or the court. If you are consistent, children will be able to understand and decode your signals in the way that players understand the gestures of the coach. Being a parent means you'll have *plenty* of opportunity to practice the family gestures!

> Sandy has saying no without saying a word down to a science. She has two teens, Amanda and Theresa, and the three of them are at the mall. Theresa takes a look at mom, then says: "Forget it, Amanda. Mom just held up the no-way sign." Sandy has coached her daughters to know when she means no, without saying a word.

A Few Words About Yes and Maybe

Yes and maybe are easier to say than no, and they're easier for children to hear. But they have their own pitfalls.

Yes is often considered a promise. If you say yes, and then things don't happen as expected, your children may lose faith in you or may begin to question their trust in you on big issues. Try "maybe," "let's see," or "yes, if we're out by 3:00" (using a qualifier) when you're not entirely sure.

Remember: It's easier to go from a *no* to a *yes* than from a *yes* to a *no*.

Maybe has to mean maybe. Maybe is fun. Maybe is let's see, let's negotiate, or let's try and make it happen. Maybe is a 50% chance of happy and a 50% chance of disappointment. When you say maybe, you mean "let's leave it open." Don't say maybe if you mean yes or no, especially if you are avoiding saying no. Say maybe and mean that, too.

Yes is yes. Maybe is maybe. No is no. Keep this simple, too.

Chapter Eight

Safety First

Almost everyone has been caught with a flat tire on a rainy, miserable night. For those who are prepared, the misery is short-lived and they are quickly back on the road, wet and exhausted but pleased with themselves for having planned in advance. In terms of parenting, unexpected breakdowns can be far worse than having a flat tire, but being prepared will make the less pleasant moments tolerable for all involved. This section will take a look at what you can do to keep the family out of the repair shop and make the ride as smooth as possible—the *how to* of creating a place of safety called family.

Nothing can guarantee what will or won't happen in a family or in your children's lives. There are lots of possible "flat tires" that can lead to temporary unsettled feelings and a sense of being unsafe. For parents it is important to provide *overall* feelings of safety and to reassure children that their family, their home and their parent–child relationship is a safe place where they can exist and, if need be, return to.

There are numerous variables that contribute to feelings of safety for children within their respective families. Here's a checklist like the one you'd use for any trip: use it to measure how safe your journey is, and to gauge where you need to top things up for the road ahead.

Family Safety Checklist

Physical Safety: Are the children in your house feeling physically safe? Threats of physical danger in the home will overshadow all other feelings. Many parents have their children join them in creating a physically safe environment in order to enable the children to see what efforts are made to keep things safe and secure. An activity as simple as changing a burned-out light bulb (and a simple phrase like "Daddy changes the bulb so you can see where you are going at night and so you don't bump into anything") will enhance children's feelings of physical safety.

Consistency: You frequently read about the value of consistency in discipline, but rarely in relation to creating a place of safety for your children. Is your home and family consistent in its values, norms and activities? Are the norms and the rules easy to figure out and to stick to with comfort? Can the children in your home guess what is next (most of the time) and do they feel that they are loved and receive limits in a fair and consistent fashion? When there are differences between co-parents, are those differences also consistent: is dad "dad-like" and mom "mom-like?"

Consistency is also about honoring promises and following through with consequences. Children are great at spotting inconsistencies—and don't be surprised if it is you being "called on it." For example, the question "Mom, if it is not okay to steal, why do you eat the grapes at the supermarket?" is more about consistency (and feeling safe) than a demonstration of a morally uptight eight-year-old!

Expectations: In the early years of parenting, being clear about your expectations of your children and letting them know what they can expect in return creates a safety net for them that will encourage learning and growth in the home environment. By early adolescence you will reap the benefits of presenting clear, realistic expectations when it becomes necessary for you to begin asking the question "What can we expect from you?"

Boundaries: Within the family there has to be a feeling of togetherness and cohesion. A strong definition of family gives all members a sense of inclusion and importance. This sense of family needs to initially be defined by the parents, and then eventually by the family as a whole, including the children. In this way, every family can draw an imaginary line around its members, within which is the family safe zone. Outsiders can visit—but the family line defines the inner circle wherein the deepest privacy and safety can be expected.

REST AREA 1 MILE

THE INNER CIRCLE

Word to the wise: Older children will question the existence of this family line if they feel their parents are sharing things that belong only within the family circle with their own adult friends or other parents. Sharing too much with non–family members can plant seeds of distrust in older children at the stage in their life when you most want them to take you into their confidence.

In addition to this family line, the family needs its individual members to feel that they have the right to privacy and to individuality, and that each individual's imaginary line around themselves is respected by one and all. This includes the use of the bathroom with the door shut, knocking on bedroom doors, showering and bathing alone (when it is safe to do so, of course), sleeping alone, the adult bedroom defined as a place to be respected, and many more indications of respect for privacy and individuality.

Knowing these boundaries allows children to feel safe and to understand that this is a family that respects its individual members.

Truth: To talk about safety in the family means to think about honesty and truth. This includes making decisions about difficult conversations: do you tell every gory detail, or just the bare bones? Telling the truth is not always as simple as it sounds. There are a number of guidelines regarding disclosing truths that can help in making good decisions that support feelings of safety in the home. Here are some:

- Silence leaves room for phantom fantasies that are well beyond the reality of the truth. For example, if kids catch wind that gramps is ill but are not told about it, they worry and wonder and imagine, and finally (hopefully) ask: "Is Gramps okay? Is he gonna die?" The truth that gramps was having an operation on a private part called the prostate gland would have been easier on them in the long run: painful to hear, but also a message of inclusion and trust in the telling. It is always best to begin by considering full disclosure, using adult language and terms, and then back it up from there to what is age appropriate and manageable for your own child.

- Keep in mind that lies and cover-ups create feelings of insecurity and will affect trust. Explaining afterwards *why* you lied will be helpful (and may make sense), but the sensation of being lied to will remain, and the issue of trust in future similar situations will still need to be resolved, regardless of how good your intentions were when you lied.

- Parenting is based on both the existing *and the developing* parent–child relationship. Telling lies in the parent–child relationship involves all the same realities that telling lies in any relationship involves, including the fact that one lie generally leads to another, that the person who lies suffers the pain of it and that the truth almost always comes out.

- Parents who lie are modeling for their children that a lie is okay if it is for a really good reason (we didn't want to upset you). This is often (and perhaps rightly!) interpreted by children as permission to lie if *they* have a really good reason (they didn't want to upset you or get in trouble or get yelled at). If you are going to make a decision to lie, beware the times you will be looking for the truth as a parent, and the future struggles of keeping things honest as you hit bigger and more serious issues on the road ahead.

- Decide in advance what is age appropriate or developmentally appropriate, before you begin a difficult conversation.

- Follow up. In most situations, you'll need to follow up with children to find out how they are feeling and what they are thinking, and to answer any questions they have. In small children, follow-ups should include discovering what they think you have told them, and then pursuing additional thoughts, feelings and questions.

- Older children may want to respond to the truth privately and should be encouraged to do so as *part* of their integrating of events into their life in the family, but not as their *only* way of doing so. Some kids respond well to journaling; whereas others can more readily draw a picture to express their response to a truthful situation.

- Children can be retold the same truth over the years with new and age-appropriate information added to eventually bring them to an adult understanding of what has taken place. Re-telling is crucial in that it acknowledges that what a ten-year-old and what a fourteen-year-old are capable of understanding and coping with is radically different.

- Telling the truth about small things will be a great base to work from when you get to the big truths! This applies not just to you and your decision-making, but also to your children, who are learning step by step how to handle difficult news, how to express their feelings and how to communicate these things to you. From smaller truths you will also see the effect of news or truths on them, and begin to develop strategies for helping them with larger issues.

- If you are faced with the dilemma of telling a truth based on an unexpected question from a child, it is important to remind yourself that a child's question does not need to be answered immediately. Once a question has been posed it is fine to say, "That is a great question! We're going to answer it at dinner tonight." This way you can take some time to formulate your best possible answer. For older children, saying, "Mommy isn't sure how much to say or what to tell you right now," may be the safest and the most honest and respectful answer to an inquiry.

Because so much of parenting is about the correcting of mistakes and errors, a climate of safety in the family takes on a great deal of importance. When you encourage honesty and trust, you are ultimately setting the scene for your children to feel safe to fail, to come home for help, to tell, to ask for assistance in the middle of a mistake, to ask for a ride home when things have not gone right in the evening and to ask for a few minutes to explain their own truth.

Regardless of how many safety checks you do, there'll still be lots of bumps, oil changes, emergency side trips, flat tires and more. You can't control everything. But with these tips firmly in place, you can enjoy the ride with the knowledge that you've created a safe home: a home you and your children can return to again and again on the long journey.

Chapter Nine

Communication

On any of life's journeys, how well you can communicate will be an important factor in the many successes and failures you will experience along the way. Understanding communication will lead to being a better communicator.

Simply put: Communication is about sending and receiving messages

Sending Your Message

Talking is generally used as the first way to try to get your message across to your children. Here is a quick-reference list of the guidelines great talkers follow. Feel like your messages aren't getting through? Run down this list to see where you may be slipping up.

- Use age-appropriate language.

- Say things once and find out what the children think you are saying (feedback).

- Tell the truth.

- Say what you mean and mean what you say.

- Try not to talk when you are feeling very angry or guilty.

- Avoid obvious traps like swearing and bad-mouthing others.

- Don't talk to your children as if they are your friends.

- Try not to yell.

- Have private talk and public talk (and topics).

- Talk less, listen more.

- Pick an approach (more on different approaches later in this chapter) and consider the long- and short-term benefits and drawbacks of your approach (i.e., nagging may accomplish something in the short term, but in the long term it will create nearly endless hassles and work).

- Think before you speak. Pay attention to those days and moments when you need a break; take the time you need to be calm and positive, especially before a difficult conversation.

When Talking Fails

Sending messages involves more than just the use of your vocal cords. When communication falters between you and your child, run down this list of ideas and reminders for help.

- Use gestures (e.g., the hand up means stop, shake of the head means no, thumbs up means "I saw that and you're great," and so on).

- Post notes and written messages for one-time reminders or messages (i.e., tape a note on the TV that says, "Today is room-cleaning day—room first, then TV!" or place a note in their lunch that says "Have a great day!")

- Hammer up permanent signs (post a sign in the kitchen that says, "This is a house where everyone helps with meals"). Point to it when necessary.

- Write e-mails and text messages to your children and talk online with instant messaging (e-cards and e-photos are fun, too!).

- Send a card or letter in the mail (yes, to your home!) to relay a bigger message ("Thanks for making my birthday great" or "At my desk thinking about how proud we were of you at graduation last night").

Receiving Messages

Everyone knows how difficult listening can be. However, what you hear in parenting is often much more useful than what you say. Listening is not just listening to the words and ideas of your children, but also learning to interpret and integrate their words into further thoughts, questions, conclusions, comments and suggestions. Listening at this level encourages talking, every parent's dream! Some of the things to pay attention to when listening are:

- their words

- their ideas

- what you think they may be trying to tell you

- their affect (their emotional content)

- their behavior—during the telling as well as before and afterward

- their body language

Active listening is quite complex and requires your full attention so that you can do the following:

- empathize

- use your intuition

- formulate general impressions

- look for ways to assist the child (guessing, adding to, clarifying, hypothesizing)

- use your knowledge and information about topics they are discussing

- use your experiences of the past with them or from parenting your other children

- focus on your reactions as you listen, using each opportunity to further create a safe listening and learning environment.

Everything Is Communication (and It Just Never Stops!)

Communication theory teaches "you cannot not communicate." The double negative is the clearest way this concept can be stated. For example, the act of *not* talking can, at times, communicate more (and more clearly) than anything else. Even the basic act of breathing tells the world that we are alive, and the silence after our last breath communicates something, too!

If we move this concept to the parenting arena, what becomes apparent right away is that one can never listen to everything—you cannot pick up every signal that comes your way, and we all have filtering processes that enable us to avoid becoming overwhelmed or over-absorbed. Use the lists above to check in on areas where you may not be paying attention to your child's broad spectrum of signals; they will help you to make sure that your filtering skills are not habitually blocking out key communications that your child may be sending your way.

Communication Is About Relationships

Communication has to fit the relationship that it takes place within. The parent–child relationship begins as an adult–child relationship and transforms through many stages into an adult–adult relationship. This growth is extremely important, because young adults who are still stuck in communication at the level of parent–child will find it difficult if not impossible to safely bring home the issues of the world that they face in their day-to-day struggles and successes. Young adults wanting to talk about issues of sexuality, drugs, political views and their own relationships as an adult in the world cannot do so if they are stuck in the language and relationships of childhood, which will not support a real expression of their own adult thoughts, opinions and realities. This creates a growing sense of distance between children and parents, and many, many parents confirm (with the wisdom of hindsight) that this separation is both unnecessary and painful; the early years of closeness are sorely missed.

Stop for a moment to examine this issue. Ask yourself, "Have we moved forward in our communication so that we are able to discuss the issues that are topical to children of this age?" If you discover that you have not, it will be worth your while to initiate discussions on topics that are now relevant to your children. Try to use age-appropriate language and ideas that will initiate real responses. For example, let's say you have a teenager who has been in a relationship for six months, and you realize there is discomfort in discussing the bigger issues of commitments, social norms, sexuality, balancing school, family and friends, and ethical and moral conflicts that may exist. As the parent, you need to be the driving force.

This means introducing new language to the relationship and addressing things in more adult terms. The impetus for doing this is strong: if you don't catch up in communication with your children at the stage they are at, the next stage will be even more difficult. The next stages of good, clear communication will hinge on the development of the skills needed to communicate today!

The opposing parent–child structure—parents talking with their small children about adult issues and concerns—is also a common communication block and equally problematic. The outcome of this unbalanced form of communication may be children with a terrific vocabulary and command of language who are stuck playing the role of "little adult" at the expense of their childhood. Children need to be spoken to and interacted with at a level that matches their developmental stage.

Listen Actively, and Relax

Know a family that you would describe as being "over-parented?" The problem likely has to do with communication, and listening skills in particular. There is such a thing as focusing too much on active listening, and doing this will inevitably make everything and everyone operate at a heightened state within the family. In this scenario, a family will begin to feel as though it is living under a microscope. Too much focus on listening, as opposed to creating better communication, actually has the opposite effect. Family members begin to seek out privacy and boundaries, and they feel invaded at every gesture and by every remark. This is particularly important during the parent–adolescent communication phase.

Listening is critical, but it must be done in balance with the overall goal of open communication. Consider carefully what you want to address, and what you can leave in the hands of your capable teenager. You aren't looking to make small issues large, or to take matters into your own hands at the first sign of trouble. This is an art and a science of its own, but taking the long view and remembering your ultimate communication goal will help you!

Don't Take All Communication Personally

It is critical to note that communication can be both intentional and unintentional. An innocuous gesture, a comment or even a glance, can be received as hurtful or upsetting, regardless of the sender's intention. Crossed wires and the "broken telephone syndrome" are common in all families. Reducing the impact of these moments requires: first, a solid base of open communication, and second, the learned ability in both the speaker and the listener to evaluate objectively.

Everyone has an automatic response of interpreting communication to be in some way about themselves. However, you can learn (and teach) the important skill of not taking everything personally in communicating with your children.

Communications cannot be retrieved; this is why this processing of miscommunications in relationships is so important. The act of forgiving (not forgetting) will need to be used in order to continue through life in today's busy and highly interactive interpersonal family constellations.

How do we avoid escalating miscommunications?

Initially, don't take things personally. Make it your habit to consider other reasons (that have nothing to do with you) that may explain a communication or behavior in others. After you have collected other rationales for what seemed to be a slight against you, then (and only then!) can you consider including yourself, still within the context of the wide variety of possibilities.

> Linda's daughter Terry came home in a miserable mood: she stopped at the fridge, went on to the cookie cupboard, glanced in the direction of the family room (still not a word spoken) and then went up to her bedroom. The absence of civilities raised flags for Linda. She thought something must be wrong, and wanted to check up on her daughter. On her way

upstairs her worrying switched to frustration: "Why does she not treat me with respect? Is it so hard to come in and be pleasant?"

The problem is, Terry was really just not in a talking (to anyone) mood; she was having a teenage moment filled with thoughts about the day, who likes who, what feels okay, what to do, not do . . . you get the idea. Terry's behavior is actually not designed to communicate anything to her mother! Linda is busy receiving messages that are not really being sent to her (or anyone else) and by taking them personally, she escalates the situation from one person's grumpy or distracted day, to an interpersonal issue!

How do we avoid this? Linda could ask Terry (checking out the message she is receiving) "Does this not talking, eating and then heading straight to your room mean anything, honey?" and Terry (respecting that she was unintentionally communicating) could help by saying, "No, mom, just not in the mood to talk." Linda can then turn off her receivers and end any assumptions that were forming.

Assess Your Parenting Communication

The first task is to find a way to describe or categorize communication in your family. This can be done by picking a metaphor that describes it (generally), selecting an activity that it is like, or even drawing it. Doing this will allow you to more objectively and fully see the strengths and shortcomings of familial communication. Over the years, parents have come up with innumerable responses; here is a sampling to give you an idea of how the exercise works, and how loopholes in communication can be defined and later addressed to create positive changes for parents and for children.

Edna is the mother of three children in a fairly traditional European-based nuclear family. After some thought, she describes her communication in the family as "the switchboard operator." She finds herself a part of nearly every communication, and is constantly directing messages from one person to the other. She sees how this began with their first child, a daughter, when her husband took the passive approach of: "You are the mother, she is a girl, you can talk to her more easily than I can." Implied in this rationale was Edna's husband's trust that she would "plug him in" whenever necessary, a behavior their daughter and her siblings also came to assume would take place over critical issues.

Although the family runs smoothly, it is a lot of extra work for Edna, and learning opportunities and chances for intimacy between the other family members are being missed. Edna also becomes aware of why she has allowed this to become her position within the family: if she pulls out of this role, she will no longer be in charge of the communication. People will have to deal with one another directly. At this moment she realizes that her husband will have to deal with tears, with children's emotional moments, and that he'll need to have a longer fuse for the day-to-day of parenting.

With these thoughts in mind, there is room for change within the family constellation, and all members of her family can define their communication goals, understand the difficulties that may arise as they set out on this new leg of the journey, and create a new definition of better.

Gina is a single mom with two boys, and she calls her communication style "the detective game." She is a naturally curious woman who loves to chat about anything and everything, but as soon as the words "detective game" cross her lips, she realizes the family communication structure is not a two-way street, and that she must make changes. Operating as the detective and interrogator is particularly unsuited to parenting teenagers, the stage Gina's kids are rapidly approaching.

Gina comes to understand that she needs to look more closely at her listening habits (developing other skills in addition to questioning), but that in order to feel safe letting go of old habits, she also must explain to her sons what information will always be important to and reassuring for her. In the end, she is able to define what she wants as voluntary communication: conversations that take place because everyone wants to talk, and because they are welcome to talk as much as they'd like. Again, Gina has found her starting ground—the hurdles she will most likely face in altering her family's style of communication are defined before the changes are instigated, and the new goal is understood by all.

Communication Checklist

✓ You cannot not communicate (even silence communicates something!)

✓ Communication is powerful: it can be the biggest problem or the ultimate solution in the parent-child relationship.

✓ The way you send your message will partially dictate whether or not it will be fully received, and how it will be received.

✓ Communication is a combination of verbal and non-verbal cues, always working together to form the overall message. No part of the communication equation is ignored or forgotten by great communicators.

✓ Talking is an age-specific and relationship-specific activity.

✓ Listening involves more than the ears.

✓ Receiving messages and making decisions about what to do with them requires thought.

✓ Doing nothing beyond "thinking about it" may be the best thing for a period of time.

✓ Communication *is defined* by the relationship it takes place in.

✓ Communication *defines* the relationship it takes place in.

✓ Make it your habit to initially assume that communication is not always intended to be about you. (Don't take it personally, first.)

✓ Communication is work. (The pay is terrible but the benefits are great!)

✓ You'll always need to figure out (define) your communication before you can fix it or improve upon it.

Part I Conclusion

- There are experts in parenting. You are one of them. Always be an expert on yourself and your family—its membership and history—and on what works and doesn't work. Use all guides, advice and experts as resources to work in a complementary fashion with your own expertise.

- Shoot for better, not perfect. Perfect is a moving target and there's no perfect in parenting, or in any relationship.

- Model roles in your parenting and be a role model to your children.

- Parent in alliance, not in opposition, regardless of the age or personality of your child.

- The journey is long. Don't be short-sighted and don't get lost in the moment. Find ways out of the moment that will help you think long-term.

- Keep it simple—find your personal three words a day for when the road gets bumpy. When it looks complicated, knock it down to the simple version and navigate in that mode until the path is clear. (Don't worry, it'll get back to complicated and overwhelming just up ahead!)

- YES you'll need to know how to say NO, and MAYBE. If you're lucky you'll get to say YES more often than not!

- Safety First. Make your family a place of physical and emotional safety where your children can securely unpack the realities of the outside world. Do a safety check regularly.

- Communication is about sending thoughtful messages and listening actively. It is the cornerstone of a long-lasting, close and satisfying relationship and it involves work. Do your best, aim for better and don't be afraid to give yourself a break.

Now that you've got the perfect framework in place for your Long Journey, you're ready to discover ten essential items to pack and why you're going to need them.

Part II

What to Pack and Why

Of course, no matter how well prepared you may be, there are always going to be unforeseen circumstances, quick turns in the road and the need to be spontaneous. Being prepared will help a lot when you are called upon to deal with the unexpected. In fact, just the knowledge that you have a few items on board to help get you through a rough spot can give you immeasurable comfort and security.

Even better, being prepared is like taking an umbrella to work with you: you can be almost sure it isn't going to rain! Keep your humor at the ready: as parents, you have earned the right to laugh about packing, because you're always doing it!

Now, let's pack!

Chapter Ten

Plot Your Course
Pack a Map

Like every journey, parenting requires careful planning, direction and destinations—for this you'll need a map. Not just any map, but one filled with clear directions and realistic destinations to guide the hopes, dreams and plans of the trip.

**REST AREA
1 MILE**

To use the parenting map, you'll need to keep in mind:

- The most important events that motivated you to set out on this particular parenting journey.

- Where other key people (co-parents) have been before they became a parent, and what motivated them to arrive here on their map.

- Where you are right now. (This is a brand new place, each and every time you look down at the map!)

- Where you are headed (you personally and you as a family).

- How to get back on course and how to set a new course when you get lost or misdirected.

There are numerous benefits to planning in parenthood; knowing where you have come from and roughly where you are headed will not only bring great security to your family, but will also supply vital tools you can refer to when things head off track. However, mapping does have pitfalls. Many people have a tendency to over-map and to get caught up in or fixated on the destination, forgetting to be an active, conscious part of each new step and stage of the journey. Zealous over-mappers take heed: while everyone benefits from a great plan, you've still got to keep your eyes on the road!

Let's start with an example that illustrates the importance of the parenting map.

> Louise and Carlos have two small children. Their youngest has just built a tower that is three blocks high! When Carlos sees this he calls out to Louise:
>
> "Louise, come quick! Gordy has built a tower! Maybe he'll be an engineer!"

It may be difficult to admit, but everyone harbors ambitions and dreams about their children's futures. At moments like this one, when Carlos (an engineer himself) sees the possibility of achieving one of his great hopes (shared with his father, also an engineer), it is very difficult for him to hang on to his best map-making skills.

As a mother, Louise is also excited about Gordy's development. She is happy to see her little one building and making things, and she would be very pleased to see him follow in the footsteps of his father and grandfather. She also knows where

Carlos's excitement comes from, because they have talked openly about his childhood experiences in his family of origin. Carlos has expressed to her how happy he is about where he is on the map they have created as husband and wife, and what destinations he has in mind for their family.

She *also* knows that the map she and Carlos have created intentionally includes some unknown destinations, in order to leave room for Gordy's decisions and input as he grows older. She understands how thrilled Carlos is about seeing his son building something, and she imagines him reaching for the parenting map in order to add a bright red destination star: Engineer!

Carlos is really enjoying this moment in his parenting. He has pulled out the map and is plotting a final destination, losing sight of the fact that it is twenty years away. Like many parents in these moments, Carlos is dreaming, but planning too far ahead based solely on these dreams is unrealistic. Saving for university when you have a preschooler is hopeful planning; signing them up for Oxford when they are three means you have left the realm of rational and useful planning behind!

Like Carlos and Louise, your parenting map is being written and updated every single day. Your map is created by combining dreams and hopes with the realities of where you are today. This is a balanced combination that gives real insight into where you're headed and how best to get there. Let's look at some of the best ways to plot your course, stay on track and avoid the most common parent-traps in map-building.

Start Your Map From Home

Each time you stop to look at the parenting map, your first question must be, "Where are we right now?"

Let's take a moment to work with this idea in your life. Ask yourself where you are right now, as you pick up this book, while you are reading this sentence. Where are you on the map that marks your journey as a parent?

Are you in "Newly-Married-Ville," planning for the parenting journey? Thinking about a spring departure into parenthood?

Are you already referring to the map? Looking over the sites of "Preschooler-Town?" or "Multiple-Birth-County?"

Having a stop-over in "Lost-My-Job-Land?"

Gripping the wheel through the peaks and valleys of "Teenagers'-Mountain-Pass?"

Pausing for a quick moment (photo opportunity ahead) at "Graduation-town?"

It is crucial that you start from the present and identify where you are. The present will give meaning to where you have come from, and assist in directing your future destinations. Knowing where you are in the present will be an anchor to the journey any time you look at the map. Our destinations are constantly in flux—ever-changing as a result of our situation in the present moment. If you don't know where you are today, you will not be able to fully understand why you are so tirelessly in pursuit of that one, engagingly perfect, destination!

The Map-Making My Parents Taught Me

How did your parents handle map-making? Take a few moments now to look back in your life. Think of this as creating a brief summary that you would share in conversation with your co-parent. The insights and ideas that come to mind will be helpful for discovering similarities and differences in your current parenting styles.

The first thing that comes to mind when you think about what parenting concepts you picked up from your parents is probably that hidden list you carry within you: the list of "things I will never do when I become a parent." You will also discover skills and traits that you would like to integrate more fully into your own parenting. This is the base from which your parenting grows—most of these ideas having been decided upon long ago, some of them as far back as when you yourself were a child. It is important to note that a negative response to a childhood recollection should be examined rather than avoided, especially because it will give you and your partner a chance to better understand how you arrived at this present moment, and how changing the path you are on can be achieved together. Positive recollections make great motivators; sharing them explains current successes and earmarks skills that will help ensure continued future success.

For some, examining your past will mean taking into account the absence of a key player or players. For example, the early loss of a parent, a history of foster homes during difficult periods, or a separation from a parent during a developmental stage will all contribute to early childhood decisions about how parenting should or MUST look. In situations like these, it is important to realize that the absence you discover is the variable that needs to be addressed. Many parents say that the reality of not growing up within a close-knit parent–child experience has paradoxically been the driving force for some very positive moments in their own parenting. Understanding the early experiences that motivate present parenting styles is important for all families in planning for the future.

Don't Forget Your Stay in Sibling-Land!

While you're looking at early influences, be sure to take a look at your relationship with your sibling or siblings. For most adults, sibling relationships will become the longest-standing relationships in their life. Generally, at the loss of their mutual parents, siblings will realize the significance of this relationship and how it started way back on their respective maps, early on in their journeys.

A great relationship with your own siblings is usually easy to reflect upon and natural to integrate into future plans. Those who have a less-than-favorable relationship with siblings will need to consider what created the difficulties between themselves and their brothers and sisters as they are now asked to teach, guide, coach and mentor their children through their own respective sibling relationships. Ultimately, looking back at sibling relationships will highlight how your parents dealt with rivalry, jealousy, differences and uniqueness in children, and it will assist you in making decisions about how you will deal with these issues with your own children.

Two Parents, One Map

Co-parents need to create a map together. This is a two-stage process: each individual needs to mark key points on their own life map (decisions that brought them to the point where their two paths converged, and places they would like to get to in the future) and then, like an intricate puzzle, the pieces must be fitted together.

If you are co-parenting, this is the time to ask your partner to look at their family history and its effect on today's parenting. Although you have your own thoughts on how they could (or should!) respond to this initial topic and the subsequent probing questions about relationships, remember that it is up to each individual to map where they have come from. Asking is okay, discussing is fine, but this is not an activity of confrontation. Once you have both taken the time to give your present parenting some historical context, have an open discussion that addresses the simple (yet complex!) question "Where are we headed as parents?"

Mapping is not a one-time exercise: ongoing planning and plotting of the family's route will need to take place at a variety of locations on the journey. Some of these are obvious and can be scheduled far in advance (birth of second child, moving to new city, signing the children up for school) and sometimes you'll be emergency planning for less-than-anticipated moments. Good map-building skills are required for both.

Remember, disagreement is good—it encourages each of you to consider your position more deeply and think about the areas where you are willing to compromise. This is where the process of mapping really begins. There are countless choices, roads to try and places to turn. The good news is, there are only four basic directions in mapping, and understanding where your partner thinks the family is headed and why (as well as communicating the same yourself) is a powerful way of aligning your forces to move forward in the same general direction together.

Moving Forward with Balance

Mapping any journey requires a sense of balance between the actual journey and the destination. Choosing realistic and attainable destinations and constantly examining and re-examining these desired outcomes is important. However, the quality of the journey itself cannot be forgotten or neglected.

When you think of planning a destination as a parent, are these the kinds of destination statements that pop into your mind?

> George is sending his kids to Harvard, come hell or high water.

> Arlene's kids are having the same luxuries she had; especially private summer camp.

> Chuck is making sure his kids don't spend their adult lives in this small town.

> Alby is certain no son of his will marry someone from that town.

Although it is important to have broad, vital destinations in mind for your children (aiming toward health, opportunity, optimism and lovingness), it is also important to remember there are an infinity of possible specific outcomes, and that *your* destination may not turn out to be *theirs*. Be cautious with this.

It helps to think about the paths your parents laid out for you, and the need you eventually felt to create your own way. For some this meant opposing their parents in order to reach their own destination, and to ultimately face disappointing mom and dad. For others it meant moving away from mom and dad (geographically and emotionally) to escape the continued pressures of a life planned *for* them, not *with* them. For others, this meant living a life planned for them, with little input, and the ongoing sense of not being where they want to be.

"I am *My Son the Doctor*"

Our society is home to countless adults who are in successful positions but are still ultimately fulfilling their parents' dreams, not their own. They have become adults who are bright and often live in the land of opportunity, but they have not been given (or have not given themselves) permission to factor in their own hopes and dreams as they matured.

It is common knowledge that as parents you can't live your children's lives for them, yet it is surprisingly easy for even the least controlling parent to fall into the trap of mapping for their child when a fundamental fear or belief of their own is involved in the process.

This doesn't in any way mean that the destination itself is horrible, but simply that it is not the real destination of that individual. For these adults, the problem is not so much that they are, for example, a doctor, but more HOW they became a doctor, following their parents' dreams and destinations rather than their own.

Those who become too invested in mapping their children's future destinations will find not only disappointments, but also a sense of regret. Not just regret on their part, but regret on the part of their children who could not, in honesty, live up to the unrealistic and unbalanced demands of their parents. This path brings disappointment, rebellion and rejection, and yet it is so easily avoided! If you find yourself having trouble letting go of a particularly special or important dream that you have plotted on behalf of your child, run down this list of reminders and tips for healthy mapping in alliance:

1. "I have to be careful with this mapping and one-destination thinking. I can get a bit carried away!"

2. "I'd like the least number of regrets possible at the end of this parenting journey. No regrets is unrealistic, and I know perfect isn't possible, but I will aim for better."

3. "I need to keep in mind that the sacrifices I am making are to support the possibility of a destination, but not to guarantee it."

4. "The journey is what counts."

Some people over-map on the journey because, like George wanting to send his kids to Harvard, they are over-invested in an outcome. Over-investing could be an indication that the parents feel their children are an extension of themselves, and that their children's successes are an illustration of great parenting. Other people overdo it because that's how they do everything—they plan a vacation with the flight information including the full airline schedules (meals planned, pilot's name noted), bring maps for every inch of a drive, note gas station locations, bank locations, hotel zones, have reservations at two or more places, and so on. If this is you, keep in mind that no matter what you anticipate, you can't control everything.

If you see yourself in this, begin to look to the road ahead to anticipate moments where your over-planning will likely become problematic. For example, your child may be a great athlete today, which you are very proud of, but may also express long-term interest in pursuing the performing arts as a career path. For you, things are going well as they are now. Think ahead: project forward to points where this tension will create conflict. Over-investing and controlling behavior on your part will be easier to manage and address today if you clearly see the looming conflict it is likely to create tomorrow.

Choosing the role of coach ("You can do it—whatever you want to achieve!") or guidance counselor ("That sounds interest-ing—Gee, I'd find out more about that.") will be of great use in keeping you involved but not in the driver's seat.

Plotting Destinations in Alliance

There is no avoiding decision-making as a parent. You are going to have to make difficult choices on behalf of your child, always looking toward the destination that you believe will bring greater happiness, and stacking the deck in favor of your child becoming a healthy and personally successful adult. How then, do you avoid over-mapping and ensure you have balanced the joy of the journey with the demands of the destination? You do this by applying a concept you are already familiar with, parenting in alliance, to your map-building skills.

Let's apply this to the example of Chuck, who has decided that he is "making sure his kids don't spend their adult lives in this small town." That desired outcome, that destination on the map of his parenting, is unequivocally children who have left this town. He is hopeful and dreaming, but he needs to work in alliance with his children, investing in the notion that future specific destinations work themselves out through discussion and the children's increasing participation, regardless of whether his particular hopes come to fruition. The "if and how" rule (how one gets to a destination is more important than if they get there) suggests that *how* they come to *their* decision to leave or stay in this town will be more important then *if* they leave or stay.

Here's how mapping in alliance works:

Chuck could say: "My primary concern is for your happiness, and if you find happiness here in this town, then that goal is achieved. However, my life experience has taught me that there are fewer opportunities for young people in places like this, and I will encourage you to broaden the scope of your imaginations beyond this little town."

Chuck wants to make his hopes and dreams known but is able to see that if he places what he wants in the driver's seat, the outcome could be quite unhealthy for all involved. Suggesting leaving town as a *possible* destination on their map avoids leaving the children feeling controlled and oppositional, guilty and behaving resentfully, or burdened by their father's unrealized dreams and seeing their choices as likely to disappoint their dad.

Eventually, of course, you will not be in charge of much of what your children do and don't do. For those of you who come by the need to control honestly, be extra cautious about what you lock into as you map and plan on the parenting route. At this point, doing better means doing less and letting go of more.

Maps Are Intergenerational

As you are no doubt beginning to see, parents' maps begin with the map-making skills they are taught, develop through their parenting years, and are essentially handed down to the next generation. Our children are a part of these intergenerational realities, not merely the product of them. Chuck himself may not stay in his little town after the children are grown, and that will become part of the journey he maps for himself, and part of the style of map-making he hands down to his children. How you plot your course, how flexible or rigid you are about your destinations, and how carefully you teach these skills to your children, will in combination make up the legacy of map-building you create throughout your life.

The Parent Planning Spectrum—Finding Yourself on the Continuum of Control

The issue of planning, over-planning and under-planning can be viewed on what I call the "parent planning spectrum."

If you are an over-planner, it can be hard for you to see this because all the over-planning makes sense to you. In fact, at times you might even wonder why other "good parents" aren't doing this much planning, too. Are you a parent who packs four duffle bags for their child's one-week trip to summer camp?

Or are you the under-planner? Do the camp counselors have to call you mid-week because your child has run out of clothes and arrived with no sleeping bag? Like the over-planner who sees more moderate planners as inattentive to their children's needs, the under–planner often portrays those who plan well as neurotic, over-involved, controlling parents.

No one is ever in perfect balance in all of this. For some, better means more careful planning, and for others better means much less planning. This is the perfect time to sit back and think about which end of the spectrum you are most likely to default to in order to prepare yourself today with tools and ideas that will help ensure balance in the future. This is about being an expert on you!

Half the fun on the parenting journey is mapping. The other half is looking at the map to see where life has taken you. Mapping a destination or a series of destinations is good planning. Getting fixated or stuck on one destination may make you miss some of the pleasures of the journey, and of raising children who grow up to be healthy and independent.

Bring a map. You'll need one, trust me. If it doesn't get you where you want to go, at least it will help you figure out where you landed!

Chapter Eleven

Remember Your Goal
Pack a Compass

It is not news to today's parent that goals are essential to the well-being of the family's membership, both children and adults. But establishing a goal or a series of goals for the family experience will take some time and effort. Furthermore, once established, family goals are easily lost, forgotten or set aside as the realities of busy family life take over. Using the model of the compass will help.

The compass is magical in its ability to consistently find direction from any location. For the journey of parenting, you'll need a compass to keep you, your children and your family as a whole pointed in the right direction, and to help you find direction when you are lost. Unlike the map, which is about planning, the compass is about staying on course, whether it is a moral-, an ethical- or a value-based direction.

Establishing North on the Parenting Compass

A parenting North is a fixed point that you can head for every single day. Not having a point that is fixed means having no real direction at all, a potentially dangerous situation to be in on this and any journey.

There are lots of things to seriously consider in permanently setting a family compass. To many parents this will sound like a lot of work, but keep in mind that it will offer a lifetime of assistance. Here are some things to think about in setting the family compass and in establishing your North, the point from which all of your directions will be measured:

North is a fixed idea that influences decision-making within your family. North is the direction you always try to follow on the journey. It's a constant. North is like a company mandate: whatever you do is always in line with that mandate. When you are off track or making tough decisions, you set your course first: aim North. North is the direction your family heads in *as a result of your parenting.* You use the parenting compass to steer your family.

Here's how it worked for one family:

> Arnie and Myra are the parents of three teenage children. Arnie thinks Myra does too much for the children and Myra thinks she is helping them by doing things for them. The couple has a map full of dreams for their children's futures and hopes for what they will achieve along the way, but they do sometimes wonder whether the three children they are raising will be ready to face the challenges of the destinations on the map. In their discussions, they realize that both of them have become concerned about how little the children really do for themselves. This becomes the

cornerstone of their concerns. Arnie and Myra need to use these exchanges with one another to settle on *their* North—one that they agree on together.

After a great deal of dialogue as a parenting team, they finally decide that their North will be: raising the children to be independent adults, or what they eventually learned to call "raising adults." This is a healthy fixed point that suits their concerns and the developmental stages of their three teenagers. This fixed spot is critical to them in using the parenting compass, that handy little device to haul out when feeling lost.

Myra hangs a sign on the fridge that says, "This is a family that is raising healthy adults"—and so the next leg on the family journey begins.

Knowing that there are stable, unwavering points and a compass to guide you is comforting for the entire family. This knowledge proves to be helpful for both daily decision-making and long-range planning. Having defined this point also means being able to parent issues on your own in a co-parenting situation, while feeling certain that there will be some degree of agreement from the other parent.

Here are some examples to illustrate how this works for Arnie and Myra:

- When they make lunch for their seventeen-year-old, they check for North on the compass and know they are off course. When they set up a rotating lunch-making schedule, they check the compass again and know they are on course. Even better than that, they've got the kids making lunch *for them*!

- The thirteen-year-old asks to do something they don't really think she is ready to do. They check North on the compass and recognize that saying no is actually off course. They teach her the skills she'll need and set up a safety system so she can start doing what at first glance seemed like an absolute no, and now is a learning and teaching opportunity. When they check the compass, they see that they're back on course—raising adults, one step at a time.

- When they come home and the kids have had their dinner and cleaned up, they check the compass for North and immediately know they are on course, full speed ahead.

The manuals they read, the parenting they discuss, the decisions they make, all are automatically checked against the North on their parenting compass. When they are deadlocked and Arnie thinks Myra is doing too much for the kids and Myra thinks Arnie is not doing enough, they can return to their larger, agreed-upon direction, and use it as a tool for drawing themselves back into alignment. At times this is more difficult for Myra because she is a doer, but every so often Arnie realizes he has to relax the role of heavy (NO!) and redirect his efforts toward helping the children become independent adults.

You can set North and learn to use your compass. North doesn't have to be profound; it just has to work for you or you and your co-parent, and your family. Here are a few more examples of North.

> Trina and Lawrence have decided that their children are going to get the truth no matter what. North started as "don't lie to your children" and has been fine-tuned to "This is a family where people can tell

the truth, which includes choosing not to answer or taking time to think about an answer."

Salonge and Ernie have decided that North is "Complete what you start." They realized how important this was to both of them, and the phrase was incorporated into everything from large concepts like "don't make promises you can't keep" to smaller details such as "we always finish the annual Terry Fox Marathon, whether we run or walk."

Darlene decided her family would be one in which North on the compass would always read, "Do your best." This was great for the children when they were young, and gave them lots of phrases over time like "Today I'm doin' the best with what I got." "Did you do your best?" became a critical question in family discussions about successes and failures. If you didn't do your best, the discussion became much more about this than whatever it was you hadn't done your best at.

By now you probably have enough by way of examples to take a moment to define your North and prepare yourself for the use of your own family compass. Remember that this is not a family exercise, but one to be accomplished by the parent or co-parents. It is useful to listen to and think about what it is you have already been saying to your children and to try and synthesize these thoughts into a North on the parenting compass.

For some couples, coming together on this will require negotiation and accommodation. Here is some advice for co-parents who find themselves dead-locked.

There can be more than one fixed point as long as they have commonality. If the fixed points suggested by each parent are in opposition to one another, it is most helpful to introduce a third party with some expertise in the area of parenting to help neutralize and resolve underlying conflict in the co-parenting relationship. Also, only establish North as something you *want,* not something you *don't want.* For example, defining the point of North as "not raising needy kids" is nowhere near as effective a goal as "raising independent adults."

The Family Compass for Kids

Once you have defined your North, you need to find ways to explain it to your children. According to their ages, abilities to understand and developmental stages, search out ways, means and the necessary language to explain it to them and to help them see its application to family life. You know it's beginning to take effect when the little ones feed it back to you! Imagine you are part of a family in which "Do your best" is North. One day you don't receive an expected promotion, and when you arrive home, disappointed and upset, your child says, "Did you do your best?"

What could be better?

When you define North, be sure to make it easily applicable and understandable: once you've done this, the sky is the limit in terms of its usefulness. Remember that children need consistency and that this will help you be consistent throughout the journey and assist in creating the safe environment you are striving for. Find a North you can live with and aspire to for the years of travel ahead.

North Can Be Large or Small

North works on a smaller scale, too, and can help in family decision-making.

Imagine that North is: *We want our home to be a place where our children bring their friends so we can be a part of their lives.*

Okay! This North sounds great. You're ready to go with it!

Then imagine that you have to re-pave the driveway. Once the driveway is done, you can't help but think, "Hey, let's re-paint the front of the house." You start picking colors. While this is going on, the kids shout, "Can't we get a basketball net?" Of course, you would prefer a house that looks fabulous as you turn into the driveway at the end of a rough day. If you check the compass, you'll find that if you paint the house and ignore the basketball net request, you are actually heading in the wrong direction. A basketball net wins until there's money for the paint job. Here's why:

- The basketball net brings friends.

- The basketball net gets kids to invite friends over.

- The basketball net means they are here and you know what goes on in their lives.

- The basketball net supports North on the compass, the direction you want to head in.

You buy the basketball net, and the journey is on course. Now the kids love this compass idea! Then they want a second phone line. You are tired of sharing the phone, too. It sounds great and isn't that expensive. But first you check the compass: *I want our home to be a place where my children bring their friends so we can be a part of their lives.* Getting a new phone line isn't heading North. A kids' phone line means no more hearing their messages, being interrupted by their friends (old and new) while you are on a call, no more taking messages and giving messages about where the gang is going, who is driving, who is calling from their part-time job about work, and so on. Yes to the basketball net, and no to the second phone line. Too bad: having your own phone line sounded heavenly.

You have to stick to your course and follow the compass. Define North for you and your family and use your compass daily. Getting lost is easy. Getting lost might even come with a new paint job on the house and your own phone line, but it's still lost.

Find North. Chart a course and try to stay on it. It's well worth the effort.

Chapter Twelve

Rejuvenate!
Pack Booster Cables

When I am asked to speak in front of groups on the subject of *Parenting: The Long Journey*, I get a lot of laughs when I hold up a set of bright yellow booster cables from my trunk. Each time I use them to talk about parenting, I think of the many Murphy's Laws of parenting, the first of which I'm sure goes something like this:

When you finally get to take a vacation, if someone hasn't come down with the flu ten minutes before you leave, and you don't have a flat tire on the driveway, the car battery is bound to die.

REST AREA
1 MILE

Parenting booster cables are indispensable for the following two reasons:

1. On the parenting journey you are certain to run out of energy, your battery will definitely be

> drained, and you will have to attach yourself to something that gives you positive energy for a boost to get going again.
>
> 2. The same booster cables will be needed to connect you to internal sources of energy — energy that you need in order to regulate and monitor your life.

Let's all say it together: "Parenting is tiring!" One more night of homework, one more fight with an adolescent, one more carpool, one more call from the teacher, one more lunch to make, one more exhausting (try and look really excited!) evening at the hockey arena and you can be zapped of that final bit of energy. Parenting demands energy, and you need to know the best sources of energy for yourself and for those you love.

External Sources of Energy

If the booster cables you need could be packaged and sold with directions, they might read:

DIRECTIONS FOR PARENTING BOOSTER CABLE USAGE

ATTENTION PARENTS:
Use with extreme caution. Please use prior to event of parenting battery becoming completely dead. Battery replacement is difficult. Do not use in the company of children.

DIRECTIONS:
Hook one end of the cable wires to you and the other to an energy source that gives you a boost. Energy sources include:

- a run in the woods, in the park, or on the treadmill
- a night out once a week with friends
- a desk tucked away in the basement for writing that novel
- an adult-only baseball league
- a painting course
- time on your own
- an inspirational book
- a no-kids-allowed project
- a morning at church
- a night out with your honey
- yoga
- a massage

Energy sources that you attach yourself to should be good for you, and help you feel refreshed and energized. An external energy boost is different from stress management or anger management. You give yourself an energy boost because it makes sense. You are not boosting your energy because you have a problem; you are doing it because you have children. Your battery naturally needs recharging because you are doing something right (parenting). This is about being healthy.

Don't fool yourself. For example, if you know that you are a workaholic, don't pretend the "desk in the basement idea" recharges the parenting battery.

Once a week. Once a day. Once a month. Find a frequency that works and that ensures that replenishment occurs *before* the battery goes dead. Do this regularly to avoid getting stuck at the side of the road. Use external sources to energize yourself, and then you will be able to give to others in a more reasonable fashion.

CAUTION: Don't wait for your kids to give back and recharge your battery. That's not their job. They may do it on Mother's Day or Father's Day, and if you're lucky on your birthday, but children don't generally do this naturally. Be preventative. Look after re-energizing on your own. There are lots of pleasures and proud moments with your children; however, these are special moments, not the everyday of parenting. Many of the more gratifying or rejuvenating rewards are way down the road in this journey. You have to hang in and learn to recharge on your own until those times arrive.

Have you ever been on an airplane? In the event of an emergency, you are directed to use your own mask, *then* give one to your child. The reason for this order is simple. You as the parent have to be functioning in order to look after your children during turbulent times. Just giving oxygen to your children will be of little help to them if you are no longer fully able to look after them. Now is the time to do this. Really. This isn't just a good idea, it is necessary for parenting effectively and over a long period of time.

How to Recharge

Time to identify some of the activities or experiences that replenish your battery: pull out a permanent marker and your daytimer, or your kitchen calendar, or your Palm Pilot or your BlackBerry. Remember to factor in your support systems of daycare, babysitters, relatives, neighbors and others in the planning. Be proactive! Replenishment requires moving things around in order to make it happen. Divide the activities and ideas you have into categories marked daily, weekly, monthly and annually in order to plan ahead. If you are in the habit of letting your battery go dead and *then* attempting to replenish, you are being reactive, which will not only limit your choices (because you are trying to replenish in a moment of crisis) but will also make rejuvenating much more difficult.

The Energy Exchange

Some events, like getting a sitter so you can go to a movie on Saturday night, might feel like a lot of trouble. But once you get out you find you really enjoy yourself. It took some energy, but you also really did get energy back—it was well worth the effort.

On the other hand, some energy replenishing sources are not worth the trouble. For example, having lunch (a lunch you feel you *should* have) with that negative friend or relative may fall into the category of "taking a break," but be wary of these relationships that take more energy than they give back to you. If this is the case, try canceling your weekly date and roam around by yourself for an hour instead. If you find you feel great—unlike how you feel after the weekly lunch—it's time to replace some or all of the weekly lunches with something that really re-energizes you. Think of this as being "energy efficient." Plan the lunch if you want to, but make sure you have real energy replenishing experiences in place as well!

Installing the Generator

Booster cables also connect you to internal energy sources.

Most parents are serious about parenting and are motivated to do a good job. Your personal motivation for parenting is what can be called the generator. It's important to identify it, install it correctly and know how to tap into it—making energy and motivation available to you when you need it most.

The generator is different for everyone. In fact, even those who are co-parenting will discover that their internal sources of energy are remarkably different. There is no right or wrong internal source, it simply exists.

Before you reach a moment of parental energy crisis, ask yourself:

"Why do I parent?"

"Why was being a parent important to me prior to having children?"

"What is it in parenting that drives me to do my best?"

"How does parenting connect to other important aspects of my life?"

"Have I made other decisions in my life (career? relocation? education?) that were designed to support this stage of my life?"

"What sacrifices and changes have I made to make this journey happen?"

"Does being a parent give me other positive feelings like pride or a sense of achievement that enhances my self-esteem?"

It is about *your* generator. It is about what gives *you* a flow of energy that helps you to complete tasks, that motivates you to do better, that encourages you to hang in and helps you to be in charge of yourself and manage your behaviors even in the most stressful or worrisome times.

Here's an example of how the generator works:

You're yelling at the kids because somebody spilled juice. You're exhausted. You are making three different dinners, and as soon as you're done it will be time to clean up and then start the frenetic bedtime routine.

You stop. You take a breath. You find energy by reminding yourself why you are doing this. If you're yelling, you are probably running low on energy and need immediate replenishment from internal sources.

At first glance this seems like overly simplistic advice: take a breather and stop yelling even though your children are driving you crazy. In truth, connecting to your generator is a much more profound process.

Many parents lose sight of why they have taken on this important role and relationship and forget how powerful their initial motivation to parent was. By consciously re-connecting to these early motivators, the ability to find energy at moments when external sources of energy cannot be accessed can entirely alter the outcome of a situation.

You didn't do this to yell or cry or fight or withdraw. You didn't have children, map, plan, read this book, alter your life and your lifestyle and give up things in your own life to risk it all at energy-less moments like these. Try and remember why you are in this experience, learn to attach to this rationale for energy and make the process of attaching to the generator within a key part of your parenting strategy. For some parents this means building in a gentle reminder at difficult moments; for others it means taking a moment at the start or the end of each day to remind yourself to have this at the forefront of your mind so it is accessible before, during and after any crisis or mishap en route. Luckily, when you hit the great moments of parenting this will all rise to the surface with ease.

Here's another example…

> Sylvia loves children and always wanted to have children of her own. She has worked successfully in an office for several years but really wishes she had chosen a job working with children. Her parents knew she wanted to work with children but necessity dictated that she enter the work force, and getting a teaching or early-childhood education degree was not a possibility for her. At this point on the map she happily has an eighteen-month-old and is pregnant again. When she goes on maternity leave, she will have her

chance to do what she dreamed of and to make up for a career choice she regrets. Sylvia has plans to stay home with her children for as long as she and her husband are able to afford it. She realizes that financial hardship and putting off the purchase of their dream home will be the cost of these actions, but is committed to the idea of being at home.

For some people this generator is about connecting to the wish of making a better family than the one they grew up in; for others it is about a lifelong dream to find a partner and create a home.

Not everyone is like Sylvia. For example, what if you didn't necessarily want or choose to be a parent? Consciously identify some of the positive ways that parenting has affected your lifestyle. Think about the different ways you have been forced to grow along this journey of parenting: in what ways have you become a stronger, better person? What are you proud of? Your generator can be represented by the tiniest, special detail of parenting. Although you never imagined you would have children, perhaps that first moment when your baby called you "mom" or "dad" is enough—consciously connecting to your love for your children may be your best generator, and it will be a major source of energy! You just have to discover it, and then USE IT!

If you didn't want to be a parent or you are not sure that you can find this generator within, keep in mind that there are lots of places and people to help you with this. Don't be afraid to get some help or to discuss the dilemmas you face. Assistance from others can come in the form of discussions with friends, parents, siblings or other parents about their motivators at difficult moments. You can also join support groups for parents, and speak with clergy, teachers, guidance counselors, social workers and other professionals that you respect in the community. Finding out how others identify and access their generators will show you how you can begin to do so on your own. Instead of the onus being on you continually sharing your personal and private concerns, keep in mind that assistance can be about encouraging others to share their successes with you. You can even integrate this into your search for greatness, as you find coaches, teachers and role models in your efforts to play positive roles in your parenting!

It's a long journey and you'll need to pack lots of things, but if at all possible, remember to pack booster cables. You'll need them to hook yourself up to external sources to get a jolt of energy and replenish, and then you'll need them to access replenishing energy from the generator you've identified and installed within. Be generous with yourself—the spill-over effect will be that you'll have the energy you need to be generous with your kids.

Remember: If *you're* okay, the parenting is okay and the kids are okay.

Chapter Thirteen

You're Not Alone
Pack a Driver's Manual

Picture this . . .

You're on the journey of parenting and there's a stop-over at your mother's place.

There you are at Nona's and your sweet little four-year-old son Ethan says to your darling little eight-year-old daughter Hilary, "You're a bitchy bitch."

Nona hears this. You look shocked, they look shocked. Everyone is shocked. (Well, okay, you've heard it all before, but you're trying to look shocked . . .)

When you were the daughter and *you* swore in front of Nona, she reached for the soap. You look over. Is Nona reaching for the bubbly bar? Will you have to deal with her (*Mom, we don't do that anymore*)? Will you have to put up with a lecture (*In* our *day the children didn't swear . . . parents didn't allow this . . .*)? Now you have to resolve children swearing *and* your mother's reaction.

What to do?

You grab the manual! Flip to the index and look up:

Bad language (four-year-olds)	page 7
Bad behavior at grandparents' home	page 12
Lecture from *your* parent in front of *your* children	page 61
Provocative older siblings (the early years)	page 11

Then, you turn to the page you chose and it tells you what to do. Voila!

Wow, what an idea, every parent's dream.

Wake up, Joe, it can't happen …

Okay, there's no such thing and there never will be, because no family, child, parent or situation is exactly like another. However, don't despair. There are lots of resources to guide you along at different points on the journey. Like a manual, they are useful when you hit certain trouble spots en route, and they are all helpful in different ways.

The possibilities are endless, but they include:

- Books
- Videos and DVDs
- Tapes
- CDs
- Sayings to post on the fridge or bulletin board
- Lectures and presentations in the community
- Parenting support groups
- Ideas from friends
- Models of parenting and schools of thought (e.g., Adlerian, Montessori)

- Journals and journal writings
- Magazines on parenting
- Internet sites and resources
- Courses

As you and your children grow, the resources you use to guide your family will change. Some parents are always on the lookout for new resources, while others tend to stop and have a look only when the road gets a bit rocky. At some point you may find that a resource has become a manual for you: it is giving you great encouragement and direction, and works really well within the set-up of your family. When you move to the next developmental stage or life event, you could find that what was a terrific manual is no longer as helpful. In this scenario, it is time to think of creative ways to apply old advice, or time to do another search.

In searching out resources and manuals to assist you in your parenting, take care not to reject any idea without first considering how it could be adapted to suit your needs. Many perfect solutions to a parenting dilemma arrive in a form that requires parent-as-expert tweaking. Ask yourself: "How can I adapt this?" and "How can I make this work with my family?" The concept of the parent as expert described earlier is of particular importance in using resources.

Let's say you read up on an idea like the "duty wheel," where a rotation takes place and household responsibilities are shared equally among siblings. At first glance you might think, "Oh, my kids would never go for that. Besides, two are teenagers and the other two are only three and five years old." Yet, with a few minor adjustments, you may realize that the teenagers can rotate a certain series of chores on a week-to-week basis while the younger ones share their responsibilities with mom. Maybe the wheel is a good idea—for now—until something else comes along and things need spicing up!

Another thing to consider: some great ideas don't work the first time you try them out. Keep in mind how long some changes take, and think long-term when using a new resource. Repetition is one of the many things that can lead to making an idea or a strategy fit. For instance, the family trying out the duty wheel will probably need reminders about the new chores. Remember, consistency creates feelings of safety, and this is another area where you can apply the ideas you have already learned. Because there are teens involved, there may also be some contagious resistance along the way—remember to parent through these moments in alliance and not in opposition. You'll need to fine-tune any new great ideas as you go along, figuring out how family and life events can best be factored into the process. These issues are all very workable—and over all, the introduction of rotating chores fosters responsibility, removes some of the work load from mom and dad, and helps strengthen a sense of community within the family. It's worth a little inventing of your own!

Find manuals. Find resources. Find things you can refer to easily and that are easy for you to read. Find ideas that fit your model of parenting and ideas that test out that model. Find theories that you disagree with, in order to strengthen your own position on parenting. And remember, when it isn't working, look again; your expertise is always a necessary ingredient in shaping the advice of others!

Chapter Fourteen

Money Makes the Wheels Go Round
Pack Traveler's Checks

Actually, you'll need more than just traveler's checks: this trip requires a credit card or two, travel insurance, a bank card, cash in a variety of currencies, an emergency fund, a slush fund . . . The family is a great place to learn about managing your money, and the small amounts of money associated with spending in childhood will give your kids a chance to make safe and guided money-making mistakes. Let's take a look at some great strategies for dealing with the hottest money issues, including needs versus wants, impulse spending, compulsive saving and understanding affordability.

Have a Strategy: Three Families and Their Approach to Spending and Saving

When young children have money (allowance, earnings, gifts), you in turn have a wonderful opportunity to begin teaching them some of the money management strategies you hope to put in place.

What follows is how three families have approached the same scenario with their children.

In all three families each child has three dollars from their allowance and three piggy banks in their room: one marked SAVINGS, another marked SPENDING and the third marked CHARITY.

Family One: The Budget Is Set

In family number one, the budget is set for the children. They are required to put one half of their money into savings, one quarter into spending and the remaining quarter into the charity piggy bank. Initially the parents supervise, but eventually the child is allowed to be in charge.

In this model, children are shown how to budget, and are eased into making their own fiscal decisions at a later date when they are comfortable questioning their parents' formula. Parents learn about their children by observing their ability to stick with a budget in the face of new and demanding life events. For example, at a time when they really are close to getting something they have been saving for, parents can be faced with resistance or attempts to negotiate the formula. Equally possible is that the child could want to donate to a school fund for a charity relief effort in spite of the fact that they cleared out the charity piggy bank for church last week. Is it more okay to change the formula for charitable spending? If so, why?

Through these sorts of discussions, children learn within the safety of their family to assume further responsibilities (making mistakes along the way) and to eventually formulate their own model of managing money.

If a parent does choose to establish the budget to be followed, remember that this should be done with the *expectation of change* (and not simply in order to be in control). Having the structure of the budget, along with the possibility for flexibility, offers a way for new lessons and learning opportunities to arise. This is a good place to adopt the role of coach, as described earlier in the book: setting goals and managing from the sidelines as situations arise.

Family Number Two: Make Your Own Budget

In family number two, the child is asked to design the formula for the division of the three dollars. At this point, if the child wants to buy a football and decides that all the money should go in the spending piggy bank, the parents must remember that they have relinquished the right to decide. This does not mean, however, that the budgeting decisions are outside the realm of family discussion—quite the opposite, in fact. The purpose of the budgeting exercise is to encourage your child in his independent decision-making, and to have open discussion about the pros and cons of his choices. This discussion should take place within the entire family—older and younger siblings will add valuable (and often frank) insights into their brother's or sister's spending habits.

The child learns a lesson as a result of his experience in his family discussion rather than as a result of limitations imposed by his parents. The parents have chosen to allow the child to make choices and to safely see the consequences of those choices, encouraging respectful discussion in a safe and constructive manner. The role of teacher works well here, allowing children to learn from their own choices and from discussions and the feedback of others, in a safe and constructive manner.

Family Number Three: Trial and Error—Learning About Budgets

In family number three, the parents know that the three dollars go into the piggy banks, but have no idea where the money is allocated by the child. There is a lot of trust afforded your child in this style—and often the outcome is surprisingly positive. Although not involved in the decision-making, the parents do have the opportunity to observe the outcome of their child's decisions—be forewarned: This can be a long and interesting process, and one that involves a lot of on-the-job training!

Providing guidance through modeling your own good budgeting behaviors is especially important when using this method because, in the absence of imposed limits, your children will take their cues from what they observe in their immediate environment. This model is an exploration of budgeting: be prepared for the disappointments and frustrations that accompany all learning processes—and for the pride your children will feel as they become comfortable with their own balanced understanding of spending and saving. This is a great opportunity for parents to see the impact of the behaviors and attitudes they may be modeling and to consider the outcome of their children's decisions as feedback for them as parents, too.

Underlying all three of these family experiences are the following guidelines:

> Talk about money and spending with your children and allow the smaller amounts used in childhood to be used for learning and taking risks.

> Be prepared to have your own spending and saving patterns questioned as you model behaviors and attitudes toward money.

> Teach and discuss the difference between needs and wants in the family and in life.

> Watch for the excessive and impulsive spender and the compulsive saver.

Modeling for Healthy Spending Habits

> Dana loves to spend time with her children and plans activities that will get them out for some fun. This Saturday Dana has planned an outing to the store, taking along her youngest child for some one-on-one time.

Dana's eight-year-old has been given five dollars from gramps. Initially Dana is busy telling her daughter what to do and what not to do. "Don't spend it all," "Save some" ("or you'll be sorry . . ."), "Do you want mommy to show you what you can buy?" As her daughter's mood darkens, Dana sees that they will get into a conflict if this parenting continues. She doesn't like feeling overly invested in the outcome of her daughter's choices, and generally works hard to avoid applying that kind of unproductive pressure. She is aware that she may be dangerously close to parenting in opposition, and that she needs to find a way to create an alliance for her and her daughter, right away!

Dana has a number of choices to make. If she encourages herself to adopt the role of teacher, she can begin to move through the store with her daughter in a whole new way. Dana can view this as a lesson on money, money management and saving—but it will mean having to let mistakes happen.

In the role of teacher, she'll need to follow her "student" for a few minutes, observing rather than directing, in order to learn more about what her daughter is good at and where she will need support. The total cost of this one experience will be five dollars: it is a well-planned and safe time for both child and parent to learn. These brief experiences function as playgrounds where valuable skills are built in preparation for the more serious arenas of the future.

The main event initially is Dana's daughter's desire to spend the full five dollars. As it turns out, this is just a passing impulse, and by not jumping in with directions ("You don't have to spend all of your money right away") Dana gets a chance to see that her daughter is fully capable of coming to this conclusion on her own. In this scenario, Dana comes to see a strength in her daughter that had previously been buried under Dana's pre-emptive parenting.

Now, Dana's daughter could just as easily have spent the full five dollars. In that scenario, Dana could simply wait until the next time her daughter wanted to buy something small in order to discuss saving and spending. This would allow her daughter to become responsible for her actions and for their consequences, without Dana having to impose a *preferred behavior* by interfering. Either way is a win.

REST AREA 1 MILE

FOLLOW THE LEADER

Letting your kids take the lead is a great way to learn about them — and about yourself, too. The idea is to use what you learn to provide leadership in their lives in the years ahead. In your life you may have been encouraged to see the act of following as negative ("behaving like a sheep"), but in parenting the act of following is quite the opposite: it is an exercise in skill-building for both parent and child!

Chapter Fifteen

This One's for Everyone
Pack a Camera

The suggestion to pack a camera is meant both literally and figuratively. One of your roles as a parent is that of photographer —or today, videographer and digitographer—keeping in mind that it's your job to make the memories, and then to catch them on film.

Like many parents, you probably sign the kids up for hockey and dance, drama and gymnastics, skating and swimming, send them to camp, take them on vacation and lots more, all in order for them to have a memorable and active childhood. There's no doubt you'll need a camera along the way!

However, it is also your job to do what I call "spotting the memories." Spotting the memories means consciously noting them in your mind's eye, and being on the look-out for those golden experiences and accomplishments in your child's life that are not necessarily photo opportunities as much as they may be opportunities to apply a bit of relationship glue.

Spot the Memories

Spotting the memories is about capturing things in your child's life with a different kind of camera. Spotting the memories is about using a camera that is not in your hand, but in your heart and mind. The lens of this camera is in your knowing glance, or concerned touch, and it is focused by your feelings of connectedness to your child.

Spotting the memories is always a little tougher than snapping a photo. You'll really need to focus your lens on your children. You'll need to center your attention on their strengths, weaknesses, challenges and fears. You'll need to be an expert on them, and close enough to them to know when the photo moment has arrived.

REST AREA 1 MILE

When a parent spots a memory and captures it, that parent gives this message:

I am watching you closely. I am close to you. I know you. I know that this is a memorable achievement or moment for you. I am recording it for both of us by focusing on it as though I were taking a picture that would last forever. And when you look up and see me, I am captured in your mind's eye, too.

Maybe you notice that your child is nervous, practicing for a big event or presentation. Perhaps you saw your child run home to see if that important party invitation was in the mail, or gallop back and forth to the phone all evening hoping to be invited to the movies. When the invitation is in the mailbox or the phone does ring, you see that happy moment and you make sure your child knows that you saw it. You spot the memory that no one else in the world would understand.

At first glance, this might just seem like a message to "know your children." It is, in fact, much more than that. This message is meant to encourage you to *act* on that knowledge of your children, and to use it in ways that will enhance your relationship beyond the positive feelings children have when their parents take an interest in their lives.

The memories that you spot don't often come by design. They result from having an intimate and conscious relationship with your children. There will likely be points in the journey when parents feel some distance from their children; having a history of closer moments will help carry your relationship through more difficult times. In parenting, this is relationship glue.

Here's a real-life example:

> Jennifer's parents think kids need to know how to swim. They research locations, figure out the cost, and sign her up. At the age of nine, Jennifer still won't go beyond the shallow end and is terrified of deep water. One day at lessons, Jennifer jumps in the deep end. No special award. No test passed or failed today. Just one of the proudest moments in Jennifer's life. Jennifer tries to play it cool. But Mom knows! Dad knows! They saw it happening. When Jennifer surfaces and looks at them, they are already looking at her.

> This is the moment. They are there, and they spot it. Jennifer is in their picture, proud and happy, and they are in her picture, when she looks up, sharing in the moment. Together they stop the journey, take notice, take a picture with the mind's eye and share it. No copies of photos available. For this one, you had to be there!

Sharing in these moments is not always about physically being there. No parent can be at every soccer game, swim lesson and school event. In today's hectic world it is also important to build in the activities of checking in with your children regularly, and to take time to celebrate great moments with them when they return home. This is also relationship glue. Spotting the moment as your child walks in the door, setting everything else aside and making time to hear about it, is spotting the memory! Being a good listener and using the communication skills already discussed in this book will even further enhance the experience of telling and hearing about these moments.

Pack a camera, figuratively and literally. There will be memories you make and memories you spot. Glue it all together. If a picture is worth a thousand words, looking up and seeing your parent or parents secretly spot a memorable moment, or having them there at home to share your excitement, is worth a million.

Chapter Sixteen

Need Help Drawing the Line?
Pack a Whistle

Like a good referee, you need to make the rules and then make sure the children know them, too. After that, you have to feel secure enough to call the plays as you see them and to maintain some degree of order when things get heated. Being a great referee, and knowing how and when to involve yourself in your children's conflicts, is what I call parenting with a whistle. If you have already learned to adapt and integrate other roles like teacher and coach, the referee should be an easy role to work with!

Sibling rivalry often calls for parents to play this role, yet the vast majority of parents loathe stepping in. Siblings do need to work things out on their own, and a bit of healthy competition and jealousy in the safety of the family home is good training for life. Arguments and heated negotiations are acceptable and necessary, but when things get out of hand (physical fights or name-calling, for instance) you will be the one who has to blow the whistle.

It is important not to become the judge and jury at this point—you want to avoid long-drawn-out proceedings, with children recounting endless stories as evidence so that every sibling altercation becomes a federal case. Children will want a trial, but the referee is not there to hold trials. The referee's job is to call the plays as he sees them and hand out the established penalties. After that, the game keeps going, and so does the journey, at least until the next penalty! The role you want to play is referee and the role you want to avoid is judge—use your knowledge of working with roles to keep this all in place.

Sometimes it is necessary to explain or re-explain the infractions and what the consequences are. At these points it is useful to have a family meeting or two to review what is acceptable and what is not, including children's reactions to the referee's call for a penalty. Treat this as a review of the rulebook. Using situations that are fairly recent as examples will help you to illustrate your points clearly. Consider this example:

> "Stefan, yesterday you were on a time-out because you took a swing at your brother that didn't connect. You can't do this when you are upset, and dad and I will always step in when this happens. In this family, hitting or trying to hit requires a time-out. We are not taking sides; we are stepping in when we have to."

The danger of using real examples is that yesterday's argument may open up again. It is important to make it clear that these are examples, and not the start of the much-anticipated trial by jury the children are still hoping to get.

The clearer the rules are to the children, the easier it is for you to referee, for them to accept your role, and eventually for them to interact with one another at moments of conflict in a healthy manner within the given parameters. Keep in mind, role modeling your conflicts as co-parents and with adult siblings in your family is important in this process, too!

For many children, just knowing there's a referee with a whistle and a rulebook helps them to stay in line in much the same way that a police crackdown on neighborhood speeding tends to slow everyone down—at least a touch. They see that their behavior has consequences and that there are parameters that they must operate within—not necessarily the parameters of best behavior, just those of fair play in a busy family with more than one child. Keeping sibling interactions in line is also about consistency and feeling safe in the family.

Let everyone know you're there to referee and to step in if need be, and encourage your co-parent to also have a whistle in hand—now you're ready to go!

Chapter Seventeen

Computer Safety for All Ages
Pack an Electrical Adapter

In all likelihood, you're already on the proverbial information highway. By now you've seen, heard of and own innumerable electrical and digital devices that make life both easier and more complicated. Safe parenting in the digital age requires a willingness to adapt and some familiarity with an entire host of gadgets: you'll need to pack an electrical adapter!

The world of technology has truly started to dominate home life. Many of the positive parenting strategies used in the past to address issues of television, telephone use and homework are now being challenged by the computer and the Internet. New questions are surfacing in areas that are unfamiliar to many parents and involve decision-making with minimal amounts of information available.

Here are some of the most common questions parents ask:

1. Is it all right for kids to have a computer in their room?

2. At what age does my daughter really need a cell phone?

3. What *are* blogs, instant messages, text messages and the other activities children are involved with online?

4. Is there really a computer-based "lingo" beyond LOL (Laugh Out Loud)?

5. Our son blanks the screen when we walk by—are we snooping if we ask to see what he is working on?

6. If my daughter is making friends with others around the world, how much do they know about us by having our e-mail address?

7. Do my son and daughter use the computer and the Internet differently?

8. Are there ways we can find out what our children are saying or doing online?

9. What are the hazards of our children posting their photos online? Is there ever a need for them to post photos of themselves?

Parents are challenged to understand the complexities of the technology and then the multifaceted social implications of online activities.

Once your children are online, they are going to be text messaging, instant messaging and e-mailing text and photos and videos. You may be surprised to learn of some of the possible outcomes of cyber-talk and Internet use beyond the obvious fact of exposure to the uncensored world of the Internet or the scenarios sensationalized by the media. As the first generation of "onliners" have grown up, we have seen the rise of new social issues closely linked to technology.

Computer Issues Beyond Our Imaginations

Many children are becoming the victims of cyber-bullying in their homes. Problems such as addiction to online gambling are also new. Children, especially those who are feeling vulnerable to peer pressure, are now making demands on their family for the latest technology: the cellular phone must be replaced with the cell-camera phone, which must then be replaced with the cell-camera-video-text-message-TV-music-podcast-phone. And though the monthly payment necessary to keep it all up and running can be atrocious, within reason these technologies *can* prove helpful in terms of keeping in touch easily, keeping your children in the social loop and making sure your children have all the necessary items to fit in with their peer group. But what does "within reason" mean in this context?

The Internet can, of course, be very helpful to children (beyond the homework rationale that so many children sell their parents on). For example, there are introverted and shy children who would have great difficulty phoning other children or joining in kid-focused groups, but who are capable of going online, messaging and interacting for hours at a time. For them, the Internet has become an important part of their social life, rather than just an adjunct to school and playgroup/sports-related activities.

Children being introduced to the tools of technology are in need of informed supervision, and parents must make an effort to increase their awareness of the issues their children are facing. For parents, the rationale for becoming users and getting online themselves is obvious. Once you yourself get online, use e-mail and all of its variations, visit and access blog sites and learn to use instant messaging effectively, you will be far better prepared to protect your children from potential hazards and to parent these issues in the home.

> Celeste and Jeremy have three children. Their eldest is a twelve-year-old named Nadia. On a typical Tuesday

night, as the evening was settling down to the chaos of bedtime for the two younger children, imagine their faces when Nadia appeared with tears streaming down her face. "I hate school . . . hate my friend Misty . . . I won't be going back to school . . . they took me off the class list for a group e-mail . . . I hate Sander . . . Misty sent an e-mail that told everyone else that I'm off the list, then someone else [we're losing track] told me that the e-mail wasn't from Misty it really was from Sander who was the sender but I had already spoken to Misty on her instant messenger and told her that I hated her," and on it goes.

Jeremy is trying to be a great dad and is lucky in that he uses e-mail at work so at least he is able to understand one part of the problem—something about an e-mail! Celeste assumed that Nadia was upstairs doing homework; she's sitting there with her mouth open wondering what is going on. No one has ever heard the name Sander (or was it *sender*?) before, so there's lots of new information, computer and otherwise.

Let's take a look at some computer safety ideas to help you plug in your adapter and deal effectively with technology-based parenting dilemmas.

Computer Safety Check for Your Home

Technology is here to stay: more and more parents are getting an electrical adapter for the journey, and you can, too! The schoolyard really does currently extend into the home, and this interaction should be age-appropriately supervised just like any other interaction.

Here are a few of the steps being initiated by parents to respond to the issues posed by technology:

1. Many parents will only allow the family's computer to be placed in a public place: they have moved

computers out of the children's rooms and brought them upstairs from the basement. Others have been lucky and smart enough to never have let them get to private spots in their homes.

2. Some parents have had computer technicians install programs (easily available) to monitor and record all online communications to and from their home computer (including instant messaging).

3. In other families, parents have begun to use the computer in ways that mirror their children's usage. They are doing this in order to understand firsthand the technological possibilities (both good and bad). Children and parents are getting online together with instant messaging, e-mail, blog sites and more. Parents are using the Internet and all that it has to offer not just to gain insight into their children's world, but also to become more effective in their parenting. Technology offers real advantages to parents who want to improve communication, keep up-to-date and understand where they need to set limits in order for computer use to remain safe.

4. Many parents now try to use the Internet and technology as a parenting tool. Imagine a text message to your daughter's phone that says, *Are you on your way home now? Clean up your room!* (Attached is a photo of the room downloaded from your phone and taken this morning.)

5. Parents now check in with younger children regarding who their instant messaging contacts are, and how well they know them, as part of their efforts to set up rules for safe online contact and to ensure that their children stick to them.

Interestingly enough, a great deal of the advice and many of the guidelines that will be helpful to parents can be found online! Yet another reason to get the adapter, charge up the computer and get in the (cyber-) game.

The journey ahead may well be guided by the "gstar world locator" and the "mapquest map" accessed in the car on your wireless Web Internet system, and parents will need to be prepared for all that this entails. (Including checking their compass to make sure their choices about technology are headed North!) Grow comfortable with your computer skills, and pack an electrical adapter; you'll be busy with electrical things from here on in. A bit of the simplicity of Love and Limits may come in handy along the way—both will be needed to make things safe and to approach the complexities that have to be faced!

Chapter Eighteen

Remembering to Remember
Pack a Scrapbook

The parenting journey is long, but it moves quickly. If you're planning and mapping, and moving through the journey at a rapid pace, keeping track of things as they happen will be a good idea.

The first bit of advice here is really quite simple. On every card, candle, frame, picture, pet rock and special gift, write your child's name and the year it was made. Right on the item. In permanent marker, the kind that lasts forever! Today you're sure that you'll know it's the one that Alan made in kindergarten, because the one Janna made had yellow buttons on it. But it's a long journey.

REST AREA
1 MILE

Trust me: the only guarantee in parenting is that you will forget things.

Another great idea is to keep a scrapbook and a journal. It is incredibly important for every child that you remember and record important moments in their lives. This helps to provide them with a sense of place, an identity and a personal history. You are the historian. Your work documenting and preserving your family's important or telling moments will be appreciated, not just by your children, but by your children's children (and their children . . .). Think of how precious your grandfather's scrapbook is to you. Or, if you don't have one, imagine how excited and connected you would feel if one was discovered tomorrow. You are able to give a sense of place—don't miss the opportunity. Your children will thank you . . . when they're thirty!

It's worth the wait.

Chapter Nineteen

Enjoy and Indulge
Pack Treats

Treats, like cameras, are things you'll want to pack both literally and figuratively. However, make sure you think beyond the simple notion of indulging in sweets, to the idea of treats as including pleasure or spontaneity.

Before you take a look at some of the many marvelous treats you can indulge in, a word of caution: don't tie treats to discipline or behavior. The question should be "Who wants a treat?" not "Who wants to earn a treat through good behavior?"

**REST AREA
1 MILE**

Don't ruin treats by tying them to all kinds of things. Making treats too complicated takes the fun out of them. Remember: treats are supposed to make the journey more enjoyable for everyone.

To make the journey a bit easier, you'll need two kinds of treats: treats for the kids, and treats for you. (They are rarely the same thing.)

Treats for the Kids

Treats for the kids help them to relax, have fun, let loose and enjoy. To have pleasure. Treats for your children are also as unique as your children themselves. A treat for the son who loves baseball is a stop at the baseball card store and a few dollars to get anything at all—don't even go in with him. A treat for the daughter in grade one is a surprise stop at grandma's with an overnight bag hidden in the back seat—no reason—just to make it fun. Treats are a drive to a special park with the world's largest swing set, or a visit to the pet store. Have fun, be spontaneous, and make it memorable! Don't just buy your teenagers the tickets for the concert, send them on the teen scavenger hunt—promising it'll be worth it. Even if they don't do their chores, make their beds, take out the garbage, do their homework on time—this is separate—this is for fun.

Treats for You

Most parents, when considering the idea of having a treat just for themselves, need to get in touch with a new mantra first: allow yourself to be selfish! Having your own treats that you don't have to share is sometimes a big part of what makes them treats.

Not only are you taking a moment to indulge yourself (and reaping the calming or exhilarating benefits) but you can also take comfort in the fact that you are modeling good behavior to your children. The phrase "mommy time" or "daddy time" introduces early on in their lives that it is acceptable and desirable to look after oneself. That life is meant to be enjoyed. They are also learning that they are allowed and encouraged to take time and space for themselves.

Of course, if this is new to your family, it is not always easy to get started. "Mommy wants time to talk for a few minutes with Auntie Ryla" is often met with comments like, "I like Auntie Ryla, I want to talk to her" or "Mommy, read me books." This may make introducing parent treats look like more work than it's worth, but try to remember that somewhere beyond this event with the little one is the day when mom and dad are going away for the weekend, alone! Couple treats!

Sometimes treats are treats because you have a moment to yourself. It's well deserved. Don't tie it to anything, just enjoy it. You're allowed.

So there it is: pack treats for you and treats for them. You'll need them, and so will they! Don't make treats complicated or tie them to other things. They're just for fun, to enjoy, that's all.

That's why they're called treats.

Part II Conclusion
What to Unpack?

Now you can prepare for the next bend in the journey of parenting by considering ahead of time what you'll need to unpack from your fully stocked travel bag.

At different points on the journey you'll need only one or two of the items or suggestions, and at other points you'll have to unpack the whole lot. Knowing what to unpack is a learned skill in parenting. Practice makes better as you move through life's challenges.

For example, there are times in your life when saying no is beneficial, and having a number of ways of doing that is even more useful. So, you unpack your no-saying skills and get to work. But one day, you'll find that saying no is no longer necessary at so many points, and that your whistle has become far more useful. Being aware of your parenting tools, and consciously choosing how and when to use them, will bring countless benefits to both you and to your children.

The next chapter will offer you insight and advice as you pack and unpack the map, the compass, the booster cables, your parenting resources and manuals, your three words, the camera, the scrapbook and the treats for the long and exciting journey called parenting.

Part III

Lessons for The Long Journey

This section will help you take the tools you have now added to your travel bag and apply them in insightful, easy-to-understand and surprisingly useful ways. You may have a map—but are you reading it? Are your kids? Learn how to pass along the most valuable life lessons to your children, and how to keep sight of them yourself when the road gets bumpy! The lessons are quick in delivery, but they take time to apply. Underlying each lesson is a message of encouragement designed to help you make the changes that will move your journey forward to better (not perfect!) at different points along the way.

Chapter Twenty

Read the Map and Teach
Map-Reading

Raising Your Children
to Be Independent

If you've come this far in the book, then you already know that the map is yours, for you to follow as closely or as loosely as you see fit. However, while you are mapping, hoping and dreaming, you can begin to talk about map-reading with your children. Think of this as teaching map-reading. Ask your children questions like:

Where do you want your life to go?

What do *you* like best about this journey of family and childhood that we're on together?

If you were the parent and this was your life map, which direction would you be going?

When you grow up, what kind of map will you have? What directions will you take?

Remember, this is the start of their journey toward becoming adults and possibly parents to their own children. Teach map-reading early. It will only enhance their own paths and choices, and the way they journey as adults without you.

Teaching map-reading is another way of raising healthy, independent adults rather than raising children who will wait for you to plan their adult life for them. The earlier they get the message that you are moving away from planning for them toward planning with them, and from there to watching them plan(!), the better the journey will be.

Read your map and teach map-reading. Even if your children don't thank you, your grandchildren will.

Chapter Twenty-One

Drive the Car and Teach Driving

Encouraging and Integrating Feedback

The way you drive is the way your children learn to drive. One of the roles of parenting is to be a role model; you can't teach your children to be kind, co-operative and respectful of others if you drive like a maniac, switch lanes and yell at other drivers. Drive the car and teach driving—both literally and figuratively—by example.

Driving the car isn't the only thing your children will watch you do on the journey. Keep in mind that all of your behavior will potentially be duplicated, or copied! Of course, no one is conscious of this all of the time; it falls somewhere between "Practice what you preach," "Do as I say and not as I do," "Children learn what they live" and "Hey, mom, tell the lady you ate all those grapes, too!" Be careful while driving through life; the walls have ears and the little ones are listening and learning. Generally it is at the most inopportune times that they will let you know they've been paying more attention to your actions, attitudes and behaviors than you thought!

Your kids "letting you know" is one of the best ways for you to see yourself through their eyes, and to catch a glimpse of what they are experiencing and absorbing from their backseat vantage point. Role modeling is important, but feedback on your role modeling—requested or otherwise—is also highly valuable en route. Find out what the "driving students" are learning and you'll know if you need to make some changes to your instructions in mid-journey.

Driving is also about being in charge, and some parents need to have this message reinforced from time to time along the way. Children who are allowed to take the driver's seat generally get out of hand: you need to be prepared to take back control in order to minimize the damage caused by and to young people overburdened with responsibilities too early in life.

Chapter Twenty-Two

Ride in the Passenger Seat

Encouraging Co-operation, Mutual Respect and Interdependence

You need to model driving, but you also need to model letting others drive. Being a passenger takes different skills than driving—in particular, letting someone else be in charge—and that isn't always as easy as it looks.

Children need to see that the roles of the passenger, the co-pilot and the driver's assistant have value, too. Always being the driver or always being the passenger, exclusively one or the other, does not offer good practice to children who you will eventually encourage to seek out an adult, partnered relationship. In modeling the balance between driving and being a passenger, you are helping your children to learn co-operation, trust in others and the ability not to control or criticize those who do things differently. You can only demonstrate this from the passenger seat.

Children need to learn both independence and interdependence and the balance between the two in relationships. Interdependence is a key to healthy relationships. Interdependence means driving and being a passenger in co-operation and harmony. Like most parents, you will see raising independent adults as a noble goal in parenting. However, don't overlook the value of helping your kids to know when and where to depend upon others: help them learn what they need to know to live in a balanced, interdependent manner.

The maintaining of one's independence and the skills to work interdependently are *both* important messages to model and to give to your children along the road to adulthood. Fostering and modeling both traits in your own relationships will help make the journey much, much smoother.

Chapter Twenty-Three

When You Get There, the Trip Always Looks Better

A Proven Expert Strategy to Help You Keep Parenting Fun

We all remember the great parts of a journey and romanticize the difficult parts as challenges that have been met and overcome with some success—mostly demonstrated by the fact that we are here to tell the story! There may have been complaining and negative thinking during the trip, but the perspective changes once the trip is over. If you can keep this concept in mind while en route, you and everyone else will enjoy the journey even more.

To help change your perspective, consider using self-talk as you go through difficult times. Read the following list and see if you can find a positive reinforcement that rings true for you.

- "One day, this will make a great story."

- "I'm sure one day we'll look back on this and laugh."

- "I know this has happened before, amazing how I've forgotten the details now—in all likelihood this will be that forgettable, too."

- "If we didn't laugh, we'd cry—better to laugh!"

- "I'll pretend I'm writing a book about hardships, and then at least I can see this as research instead of a really bad week."

There are two great children's books that illustrate this point and help the whole family maintain a more positive outlook. The first is an easy read called *The Berenstain Bears Go On Vacation* (Stan and Jan Berenstain). In it, the family has had a terrible vacation out in the woods, but has a great time enjoying the pictures that retell their vacation and preserve their memories.

The second book is called *Something from Nothing* (Phoebe Gilman). Its message is that even if something special is lost, torn or gone forever, its memory helps us to tell a great story. Both books will help children share in your ongoing efforts to maintain a positive outlook on the journey. Remember that these are resources that require the parent as expert. If they don't fit for you, try finding some that do—maybe a song or a poem—keep the search for these family resources ongoing!

Really, on the long journey called parenting, when you get there, the trip always does look better. No, really, it does! Tell yourself this: *One day this will be a great story.*

Try it. I promise, it works.

Chapter Twenty-Four

Program First

Creative Solutions to Common Discipline Traps

In parenting there are things you can do that make the journey easier and allow you to spend less time disciplining and punishing. I call this programming first, and like to see it as the prevention of negative parenting. Simply put, parents who are good programmers need to discipline less often. Here are some examples of common discipline traps and how to work with the notion of programming first.

Example I: Pre-schoolers and the Jacket On

It's time to put on your pre-schooler's jacket. If your pre-schooler knows "flip flop over the top" (a fun way to put your coat on), you call out, "Flip flop over the top" instead of "Put your jacket on or we won't be home in time for a story . . . blah, blah, blah."

They lay their coat down on the floor, stand behind the collar of the jacket, slip their arms straight into the sleeves, and then send the jacket overhead and, like magic, they're ready to go!

Example II: Two Kids and the Chocolate Bar Split

Two kids are splitting a chocolate bar. One breaks it in half. The other picks the piece he or she wants. You're out of it. Stay out of it. You have programmed first to avoid disciplining, so let it be.

This scenario is much easier than you splitting it and hearing: "You gave her more!" or "Mine's smaller!"

One splits, one chooses, everyone is happy and you're out of it.

Example III: The Family Car Trip

It's car trip time for the family. The parent who takes along an in-car VCR, books, games, songs and/or books on tape, has three distinct seating arrangements, brings a battery-operated car light, knows five license plate games, and so on, will generally be doing a lot less disciplining and punishing (and complaining). The children are asked to entertain themselves to the best of their ability, and the parent is relaxed and ready to program ahead to avoid the moments where discipline would become necessary. Parents can change the course of their child's behavior through activity rather than discipline or other less healthy choices. Programming first really works.

Parents who don't program first will often find themselves saying, "Quiet! Can't you kids entertain yourselves?" and feeding the kids sugar and junk food to keep them *happy.* With preparation in the form of programs and activities, children are still expected to entertain themselves; however, they are given structure and organization on the trip.

Programming requires good ideas, good timing and realistic expectations.

REST AREA
1 MILE

Realistic expectations show up a lot in parenting and programming: with realistic expectations in mind, you can significantly reduce the need to discipline your children.

Example IV: Planning for Kids: The Dinner Out

Let's take a look at programming before disciplining as it applies to making dinner plans for your family. For example, making plans for your teen or your pre-schooler to see the grandparents on a Saturday night at 8:30 potentially creates issues that could easily have been avoided. Programming for your teen means keeping their social needs in mind, too. So, for most teenagers 8:30 Saturday night dinners with the grandparents are out. In the same way, programming a family dinner any night at 8:30 for your toddler means you've traded being home in bed or getting ready for bed for a completely unrealistic activity and one doomed to failure. That failure is about you and programming, and the disciplining that likely ensues at 9:00 p.m. could have been avoided with the greatest of ease.

Sometimes programming is also about saying no to others, even your own parents, keeping in mind that dinner at 5:30 p.m. might work because it is a better program for teens on Saturday night and for pre-schoolers in general. Grandparents might need a bit of Love and Limits, too!

Programming before disciplining requires a keen interest in the lives and activities of your kids. Programming is learned—and you can get ideas in lots of places. The library, the bookstore, the family next door, the video store, the Internet and the kids themselves are all resources for loads of ideas and suggestions.

Things are getting better when it comes to pre-empting and preventing or avoiding the need to discipline. For example, years ago, crayons were a no-no at the restaurant table. Today, the host hands them out to the kids or gives them to everyone to decorate the butcher-paper tablecloth. And the doctor's waiting room has toys and fish!

REST AREA
1 MILE

HELPFUL SOCIAL PLANNING HINT FOR THE
PROGRAMMING PARENT

Be hopeful when you plan. Count on being there.
Count on being as punctual as is humanly possible.
Optimistically pick dates, times and locations, and
pencil them in—then carry an eraser just in case.
Try to call these the OTA (optimistic time of arrival)
instead of the ETA (estimated time of arrival), and
the OTD (optimistic time of departure) instead of the
ETD (estimated time of departure), just to keep yourself in check.

Reality has its own time-frame. Being ultra-realistic
about your OTAS and OTDS will teach those around
you to work with some flexibility as well. A seven
o'clock reservation to meet others (especially if you
are a family with three small children) is an OTA and
not an exact science, no matter how hard you try.

Loosen the reins! Select reasonable OTAS and OTDS,
and aim for better each time.

Example V: I Act the Way I Feel: Programming Feelings through the Journal and the Feeling Board

It is not uncommon to be disciplining children at moments when
they are badly behaved only to find out that the root of the
behavior doesn't warrant discipline at all—more likely a hug or
a hot chocolate! But how do you decipher bad (disciplinable)
behavior from reactive, emotional behavior? Watch your children
for changes in behavior involving worry or stress. Remember
this maxim: children often act the way they feel. You, like many
people, will likely become focused on the external behavior you
see before you consider what is going on internally.

As parents, you can pre-program for these moments by introducing (early on) ideas like a journal or a feeling board, or in some cases a punching bag or balloon. All of these are designed to help children express rather than act out their more difficult emotions. Be forewarned: it is far easier to use these methods if they are introduced as part of the family *before* major crises arrive. This helps to avoid the pitfalls of escalation that take place when efforts to discipline are unproductive or in fact creating greater resistance and more reactive behavior in your children. Remember to introduce these ideas as ways of getting *out of* trouble in order to create the alliance you hope to have in your parenting.

For example, your youngest child is having a tantrum. Instead of reacting to this with time-outs and other discipline techniques, you ask the child to head over and pick the feeling they are having right now from the drawings by the kitchen table and put it on the fridge door under a magnet. Imagine what you could learn in that moment!

The family feeling board can be a collection of pictures (happy people, angry people, crying kids, sunsets, puppies, and so on) and colors (sunny yellow, red hot, and so on) or just simple drawings styled with different emotional expressions. Some families now use the "emoticons" listed online in instant messaging systems as a source—a bit easier than having to come up with your own symbols and another way to put in place the earlier suggestion that you integrate technology into your parenting.

After using the feeling board for a while, some children will just come home, hang the feeling on the fridge, point and head upstairs to their room. You'll think, "Wow, that could have been an argument," as you head upstairs to congratulate them for having the courage to express rather than act out their feelings (reinforce the positive) and to find out how you can help with whatever it is that is causing the feelings.

Older children need to have more privacy at these emotional moments. You can suggest that they go and write or draw at their desk and then discuss or share their feelings, if they'd like. Your hope is that they will use this as a way to express themselves in the future, and choose the journal rather than engaging in be-havior that you will be tempted to discipline as a way of letting you know they are having a difficult time.

Start the search for programs early. More programming means less discipline. Remember, you are trying to get your kids *out of* trouble, not into trouble, and you are trying to be creative about helping them avoid trouble in the first place.

Chapter Twenty-Five

Use Your Mirrors, Always

Understanding Patterns So You Can Spot the Problems Before They Happen

Mirrors are handy little things. Parenting mirrors enable you to see the past and absorb its meaning and implications while still moving forward (a.k.a. the rear view mirror); parenting mirrors also help you see the world around you clearly (a.k.a. the side view mirrors) as you cope with the present and plan for the future. Reflecting on the past and building a context for understanding and interpreting the experiences you are having now as a parent is very valuable. Using your parenting mirrors in this way will enable you to begin to see roadblocks and pitfalls ahead, based on patterns you have noticed in previous successes and failures.

Keeping in touch with where you have been will also allow you to see how far you and your child have come. This results in a sense of accomplishment and a feeling of satisfaction: you can really see that things are moving forward in your lives. Here's an example of using the rear view mirrors to move forward on the journey.

> When Chris was five years old, his mom and dad signed him up for soccer. His first team sport. Chris didn't want to go. He cried, he stood on the sidelines, he stomped his feet. It took him four games to get into the swing of things, and after that he was fine. Mom and dad thought this was because it was his first team sport.

> Hockey season came and, surprisingly, Chris was once again in tears. They both pointed out to Chris that this had happened in soccer and that everything had turned out fine, so why the big deal now? It wasn't until game six that Chris seemed to get into the swing of things, and then, once again, he was fine. Mom and dad thought this was because he had never played hockey before. Grade one came up and he was to go to school (the "big school"). Chris cried and didn't want to go. This lasted about ten days, and by then he had adjusted.

> After the first day of staying at grandma's for a week-end, the first day of summer day camp and a few other events in Chris's life, mom and dad signed Chris up for karate class. Mom said, "Oh, let's not go out for dinner after the first karate lesson, you know how hard these firsts are for Chris." Dad understood mom's new sense of planning and agreed that they should take a lesson from the patterns of the past and focus on making things work better for Chris.

In this situation both parents reflected on the past (Chris's difficulties in starting anything new) and redesigned where they were headed based on this reflection. Their expectations of Chris became more realistic. If firsts are difficult, working with that will make more sense than ignoring it or just hoping it goes away. Working with it includes developing realistic expectations, and implementing a family way of aiming for better.

The idea of using the parenting mirrors is also to learn from your successes and use them to drive forward, too.

> Aida's parents saw she was having trouble in grade two. In a brief discussion with the teacher it became obvious that the class of twenty-nine kids was a bit much for Aida to figure out, and that the teacher was not going to be able to help much with Aida's social adjustment. Aida's mom decided to take a chance and go into Aida's class as a volunteer once a week. The teacher was highly supportive of this initiative on mom's part and welcomed volunteers, already setting the scene for possible success.
>
> While her mom was in the class, Aida was able to go about her regular business in the room, and Aida's classmates thought her mom was great. Having a mom who came to school made Aida special and as things worked out, Aida's mom provided the children with some of the attention the teacher was not able to give during a busy morning.
>
> For Aida's mom, being in the class gave her an opportunity to see some of Aida's struggles and to work with Aida in the social choices she was making. This worked well. Mom used the time to get to know the players and to be a better listener for Aida. With her

experience in the classroom, she could actually know which choices to encourage and which dilemmas Aida could sort out on her own. Their discussions centered around encouraging Aida to make choices that would result in friendships rather than feelings of exclusion. Mom found herself in the role of coach and guidance counselor for Aida as she assisted from the sidelines.

In grade three, Aida joined the Girl Guides. After one week, Aida was already feeling overwhelmed and raised new concerns that everyone had friends and that she wasn't really liked by anyone. Aida was ready to drop out. Rather than wait a prolonged time, Aida's mom volunteered to go on the initiation weekend overnight with the group as a volunteer. Just as she suspected, Aida was fine in the group but needed a mom who knew the girls and could help her organize herself socially into the group.

Aida's mom was comfortable in playing a role from the sidelines, coaching Aida in a supportive and encouraging fashion. The weekend away supplied her with the same kind of information she had gained about the classroom, and enabled her to be helpful to Aida in the weeks to come. Aida's mom did not become a Guide leader, because what Aida needed (based on successes from the past) was a parent who could assist her by knowing all the players, not one who was stepping in to take over.

Becoming a Guide leader could have jeopardized the balance her mother was trying to strike between helping Aida and letting Aida figure things out on her own. Aida's mother was also able to see that Aida had needed her a lot in the classroom, but a bit less in the Guides group. Aida quickly learned to better describe social dilemmas she faced in new groups, and, as this developed, her mom helped her with less and less direct involvement.

Aida's mother and eventually Aida herself became comfortable looking in the rear view mirror as they moved forward to new and challenging social, educational and recreational experiences. Eventually they both looked back on the grade two class, the Guides and other experiences to assist them in moving forward with realistic expectations and social goals.

The idea of reflection is helpful in many of the journeys life has to offer, including that of parenting. Ultimately, reflection on the past allows you to be better able to plan for future experiences with realistic expectations and outcomes for yourselves and for those you love.

Chapter Twenty-Six

Consider Other Modes of Transportation

Different Parenting Styles You Can Adopt to Deal with Parenting Conundrums

Going really fast on a bicycle and going really fast in a racing car are, obviously, vastly different experiences. Likewise, choosing an appropriate mode of transportation as a parent will radically change your experience. What do I mean by mode of transportation?

Your mode of transportation is the style of parenting you adopt in any given situation. When faced with a problem, do you automatically feel like rushing through screaming: "Rush! Hurry! Put your foot to the gas!"? If this is one of your styles, you're on a speedy motorcycle, possibly heading down the road without a helmet, taking the turns wildly, and forgetting to check out who's along for the ride. On the other hand, some parents drift through situations, even demanding or dangerous ones, as though sailing a boat on misty waters, floating, not realizing it's time to start the motor up and head for shore!

Are You on a Motorcycle, a Sailboat or a Bulldozer?

Many parents find themselves relying on one mode of transportation for most situations, thinking that this is simply who they are, and that children will adjust. This is not true. Children will be able to see when you are motorcycling through a situation that calls for a calmer parent, and when you are drifting through a situation that requires a quick and speedy direct ride.

The more parenting styles you have at your disposal and the more inventive your styles, the better for everyone. In transportation terms, riding a hot air balloon through a situation is very different from driving a bulldozer—think options! It is very easy to get stuck in a particular style of parenting. Taking a moment to consider the endless possibilities now will give you some healthy options to draw from in future moments of hectic activity or crisis.

Here's an example of successfully changing the mode of transportation.

> Elaina's son Daniel was suspended for smoking in front of the school and she was called to come and pick him up. She frantically rushed to the school and marched into the office to collect Daniel. She started off by grounding him for two months, then demanded that he stop smoking, improve his grades, get a part-time job and do four chores a day to help his mother out. This was all in the first three minutes, as they were leaving the school.

> Daniel walked out of the school, lit a cigarette and left his mother waving and pointing her index finger at him in the parking lot.

> Elaina, with all good intentions, decided she would drive quickly into and through this experience. Her pace was guided by her feelings of anger and worry

about Daniel, and her feelings of embarrassment about his actions and how they reflected on her as a mother. Her initial transportation choice was a motorcycle at high speed. Elaina's choice was over the top, and not well suited to either the situation or the developmental stage of her son. In fact, she already knew Daniel smoked and until this happened had been paddling her way through it, cautiously suggesting and encouraging him to give it up.

Once Daniel walked away from Elaina, she realized she needed to change the mode of transportation. She knew things hadn't gone well, but also that she could change the present situation and possibly the outcome. The school was already driving by suspending Daniel, so the overdrive approach was beyond the call of her parenting duty. The tandem bicycle approach came to mind: it offers the chance for some alliance.

Considering alternatives and thinking in these terms allowed Elaina not only to calm down, but also to assess where she was going wrong and think about ways she could re-approach Daniel with greater success.

You may discover that you aren't choosing modes of transportation for their speed, or to accommodate an in-the-moment emotional response. Perhaps, for example, you have chosen to cruise through this developmental stage on a bus. This parenting style has its strengths and weaknesses; the bus is unwieldy and difficult to maneuver, but has room for lots of people, including all their opinions and thoughts for the journey. It is a style of parenting that encourages stop-offs as opposed to speedy arrivals, and communal experiences and even decision-making rather than unilateral edicts. Using the bus metaphor is fun, but ultimately it describes a model of consensus in your parenting that, like all methods, has to be only one of a number of modes of transportation.

IN-FLIGHT PARENTING

Over time you will find that you can fine-tune your parenting styles using modes of transportation to describe them. Do either of these describe the parenting style you find yourself using most often today?

1. The Plane, a vehicle that moves quickly to get the family from point A to point B with speed and accuracy.

2. The Helicopter, a more personal, easily maneuvered and rerouted mode of transportation that encourages an overview landing here and there to check things out.

Both have flight in common, yet each a style of its own!

Building a Transportation Depot: The Bus, the Bulldozer and the Quiet Little Canoe

After a quick glance, it is common to discover that you can define yourself by just one of these modes of transportation. You may think of it as, "Yup, I'm a bus kind of parent, always in a group for this or that, working with others, letting someone drive, running my life by consensus" or "That's me, driving through life on a motorcycle, rushing from one spot to another, happy on my own until someone calls me on it." You could also have an insight or two about a co-parent or your own parents: "That's me, daughter of a canoeist, and wife of a bulldozer."

Rather than thinking of this as "don't be a bulldozer" or "I have to stop taking that bus everywhere," try to think in terms of choice. You have the bus down pat, now what alternative forms of transportation would work best for this part of the parenting journey? With a spouse, you can think in terms of "we've got the bulldozer if we need it, what other modes of transportation are available that we can learn to use?"

Try using the language of transportation to work your way out of old patterns into new ones.

> I always do this alone on a motorcycle. I'm getting on a bus with others for support and friendship.

> I'm asking Maryanne to get off her speedboat and try riding a bicycle for two with me through this problem.

> Annie always drives this rollercoaster and I need to ask her to join me in the canoe. I think I can paddle and steer us through this.

> I do everything on a bus by consensus, but this time I'm riding a motorcycle through it. I know what I want and need and where I'm going. Let's move it. I'm driving.

Stuck? Consider this as a way out and a way in. Changing the mode of transportation changes the entire journey for you, your children and your co-parent. Drop by the depot and select a vehicle that suits you, your children and the situation at hand. You'll be glad you did.

Chapter Twenty-Seven

Choosing by Elimination

Embrace Your Failures and Become a Better Parent

If you are able to view mistakes as ways of eliminating options and getting closer to the right choice, you'll save yourself a tremendous amount of grief and pain that comes from reviewing the past, playing the should-have game and standing still instead of moving forward.

> **REST AREA
> 1 MILE**
>
> Understanding that mistakes contribute to an eventual positive outcome allows you to integrate them into your wealth of experiences; mistakes actually encourage forward movement!

Mistakes are real, they are everywhere in parenting, and they will happen. Find a place for them and a way to allow them to contribute to your future success. At least, learning from your mistakes means not making the same ones over and over again! It would be hard to justify continually making a right-hand turn at an intersection when you know that the last five times it took you to the wrong place.

Don't be afraid of mistakes; learn from them, and try not to repeat them. Remember that in making mistakes you are modeling how to cope with that fact of life for your children—including being hard on yourself and trying to get to perfect. The children are watching: what would you like them to learn?! Make the most of your opportunities to teach them that making mistakes is okay and that avoiding the same mistakes over and over again is a good idea on the road to better.

Chapter Twenty-Eight

Book Adjoining Rooms, Regularly

Keeping the Romance Alive—Seriously!

Parenting is not a very romantic journey. In fact, it's not really a couple's thing to do. Sure, you are both there, both involved, but the activity of parenting is that of two adults, rather than that of two intimate lovers and partners. Although, interestingly enough, it starts as the opposite! Couples who are aware of this make time for their relationship as husband and wife, friends and partners, while they are on the journey of parenting.

Relationships should grow and change as people parent together. By making efforts to understand how each other experiences the myriad failures, successes and unexpected occurrences of parenting, relationships are more protected from getting lost in the shuffle of busy family life.

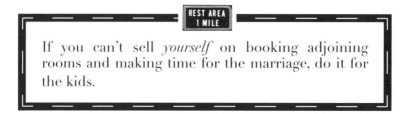

If you can't sell *yourself* on booking adjoining rooms and making time for the marriage, do it for the kids.

Booking adjoining rooms, or anything else that will support and secure your couple relationship, not only enhances your experience, it is good for the children. Aside from the overall benefit to children of having happier parents, it allows children to see that mommy and daddy time is also husband and wife time, and reinforces boundaries between children and adults that keep things in working order. Besides, while you're in your adjoining room, they're in theirs, learning to work things out with their siblings. (Bring the whistle, just in case.)

Tip: At some points on the journey it will be best to forget about adjoining rooms, ask someone else to be in charge for a few days, and just book a vacation on your own.

Remember to set aside some space that is devoted to your adult couple relationship. It really is good parenting!

Chapter Twenty-Nine

Making Side Trips

Clever Tips for Keeping Your Life Spontaneous

Sometimes you have to let go of your focus on the destination in favor of a side trip or two. Curiously enough, side trips often turn out to be the most memorable part of the journey.

Successful side trips require letting go, and this is often what makes them hard for parents to handle. Side trips are not small outings you plan; they are surprises, mistakes and great accidental finds that you stumble upon.

REST AREA
1 MILE

You are, for once, entirely on course. The family as a team is buzzing along, headed straight for the next long-anticipated destination. Suddenly, you spot a lovely sunset trail meandering into the woods—do you make time to explore it? Do you give yourself permission for a possible side trip, or do you rationalize continuing on and sticking to things as planned?

As you decide to take side trips, you'll have to keep the direction of the overall journey in the back of your mind. This will help you to keep things on track and give you the confidence to explore and possibly even allow yourself to get lost.

Here's an example of a mom who liked side trips and was willing to take risks with them in the context of her parenting.

> Sylvan is the mother of a ten-year-old named Marta. Marta has been coming home frustrated from school and Sylvan has been pressuring her daughter to keep doing her best—then Sylvan suddenly decides that it's time for a complete change of pace. With no planning at all, they are off on a side trip. Sylvan has decided that tomorrow is a day off for herself and her daughter. Generally Sylvan is fairly strict about going to school and Marta takes school quite seriously, but Marta decides that if her mom is excited about spending the day together, then she is too! (She has learned to expect the unexpected.)
>
> Sylvan and Marta sleep in, hang out, go for a walk, go to the art gallery and take in dinner and a movie. Next to the art gallery is a restaurant and they decide to try it, even though they have never eaten this food. (A side trip within a side trip!) The restaurant is fabulous, and becomes a place they will eat at time and time again—it becomes what they'll call "their restaurant."
>
> Marta knows she'll have extra homework tomorrow, and that Sylvan has a plan for mother and daughter to catch up. When Sylvan asks Marta, "Was it worth it?" Marta responds immediately with an enthusiastic "You bet it was!"

Remember, like Sylvan, at these points you're not teaching something, reinforcing something or working with saying no. You're just having a spontaneous experience that celebrates the unexpected. You are modeling how to deal with unplanned experiences, and how to be fun, adventurous or even just a bit naughty.

Don't worry about when the children ask to do it again tomorrow; you've got a whole variety of no's to put in place, and a compass to find direction. In fact, this is where being able to say no really comes in handy. It will give you a way to freely take these side trips with the knowledge that you have the parenting skills available and accessible to help you to get back on course.

Tomorrow we'll be eating our vegetables, but tonight, dinner is ice cream!

Chapter Thirty

Three Right-Hand Turns
and We're Home

Peace of Mind In an
Ever-Changing World

No one parents in a bubble. The outside world, and in particular your children's experiences of that world, need to be woven into your family experience.

The parenting journey will take you and your children to innumerable locations, some bland and others that are highly amusing. Among the people you meet along the way, none will be more stimulating than the other families you'll run into and experience at various points. As parents, you will want your children to be secure in the knowledge that they are able to venture into the world and then return home with their new life experiences—what I call the Three Right-Hand Turns.

REST AREA 1 MILE

From the moment your kids journey out the front door of your home, no matter where they head, home is always just three right-hand turns away.

Encountering other families means looking into how other cultures, religions and individuals form this primary group called "family." A few minutes in a family where there is a rigid structure to TV, telephones, computer use, meals and bedtimes will stop some visiting children in their tracks. As will the first time the children of a highly structured home eat dinner with a family where butter in each others' hair and ketchup on the ceiling is considered irrefutable proof of the best meal yet. Difference and variety are out there in the many, many forms you can call family.

Children will take things they experience in other homes and present them to their parents in hopes of influencing things on their own behalf. "Alex is allowed to buy anything he wants with his own money," will be the story you get. And it is likely the truth. But what you are not hearing is that Alex has a job on Saturdays and must put away half of his earnings before spending the rest as he chooses. At times it will seem to you that everyone's children are allowed to stay up later, stay out later, spend more money, do no chores, receive twice the allowance, play video games and probably pilot their own jet planes.

Children will compare and contrast. The trick is to encourage this without feeling challenged by it. You *may* wish to alter some family structures when you hear of inventive and helpful strategies other families use, but your bedtimes, for example, remain decided upon by you.

**REST AREA
1 MILE**

Help your children understand from an early age that your house is not run by a neighborhood consensus model, but that you are open to hearing what others are up to. This openness leads to questioning, but questioning does not always mean changing the way things are done. There is the *possibility* of change, not the *promise* of change, in all discussions.

In professional circles, this is viewed as developing a secure home base within which the family can operate, question, dialogue and discuss, with the possibility of change. Children need to see the family as a place of security where new ideas enter, possibilities exist and changes take place, and where they have a voice to participate.

The striking of this kind of family experience means that children will venture out and then return to the home base as many times as they like. They head into the unknown (for an hour, a day or a school term), experience the outside world, and then, in an instant, abandon the path ahead (make three right-hand turns) and find themselves back right where they started. They understand that they always have a home base to venture out from and return to—three right turns and you're there. In many ways these experiences can contribute to the notion of building a place of safety.

Bringing It Home: Change Is Good for You

Remember to take a moment before discarding a new idea your child brings home or one you discover inadvertently while out with others. When you feel you have struck a delicate balance with your family, it is easy to become resentful of intrusions that disrupt this equilibrium. Yet, once the challenge of status quo has been addressed, parents frequently discover that the ensuing change has been a long time coming and is good for all involved. Here is an example:

> You, your kids and a friend stop for coffee and treats and your friend says, "Oh, we just let the kids get their own table."

> You stop for a second. Your children have never eaten a piece of food or had a drink you didn't touch, cut up, unwrap or share. And yet, since you're willing to give it a try—it turns out they're fine!

Next time they're waiting for you to unwrap the sandwich, stick the straw in the drink box or feed them, you realize it is time to say, "Honey, I think you can manage this on your own."

Repeated Disorder Becomes the Natural Order

The family, as with any organized group, will operate on the principle that repeated disorder becomes the natural order of things, and it will often be an outside force that challenges a notion and moves the family to a new and better equilibrium.

> Little Joey eats dinner with his mom and dad and the baby every night at 7:30. His mom gives him a snack at 5:30 to hold him until dad gets home. One day he is finally big enough to go to his friend's house after school. By 5:30 he is getting a bit hungry, and asks his friend what time his dad gets home. His friend tells him that his dad gets home after nine o'clock. Joey asks if it is okay for him to change his mind about dinner and to just go home. As he is speaking, his friend's mother calls them to dinner. Joey is confused when they get to the dinner table and his friend's dad is not there. Joey realizes at that moment that *this* family eats dinner without the dad being home, and he's amazed.
>
> The next night he is back at home and mom is wondering what is taking dad so long to get home. Joey tells her that she doesn't *have* to wait, and that if she wants, they can just go ahead and eat the way they did at his friend's house.
>
> In doing this, Joey is pointing out to his mom that the repeated order they experience as a young family is

in fact a repeated disorder, and that other possibilities exist. Mom is willing to consider this, and to entertain the notion that Joey has left home, made three right-hand turns and come back with valuable information. In fact, she wonders why they are waiting, considering the effort they go to with the snack, the late bedtimes, the bath never being got to and all the other things that suggest eating without dad, as odd as it feels at first, makes the most sense!

As your children age, the influences of the outside world increase. Friends, the media and a host of other influences will compete with parents and family in how they shape their lives. Although it is important to acknowledge that the early experiences of childhood are most influenced by the family unit, current thought sees the major influences of teens as their peer group.

REST AREA
1 MILE

Peer influence is not always negative. Peer pressure can contribute to kids smoking, but it can also motivate kids to leave a party before trouble begins.

Teens will need to navigate their way through this period, and they will challenge and question their own family life, especially the limits set on their freedom to express and do as they please. Knowing that the family can withstand these challenges in a healthy way will not only encourage parents to have faith in the notion that with three right turns the child is home again, but it will also give teens the flexibility they truly need to negotiate those tricky years. Near-adults need to know they are allowed to question and challenge the family with the possibility, though not the promise, of change.

Chapter Thirty-One

Take Your Hands Off the Horn

How To Stop Yelling, What's at Stake and How to Find Support

If it isn't life-threatening, if the house is not ablaze, if it is not an emergency, or the child you are yelling to is not half a mile away, then yelling is the wrong choice in parenting. Yelling, although a common pothole on the road, has to be minimized and eventually brought to a stop in order to maximize the positive effects of the rest of the great parenting you are doing.

Yelling directly and negatively affects the way children see themselves and how they feel about their life and their place in the world around them. Yelling is also bad for parents' self-esteem; it is generally a behavior they are ashamed of, yet find themselves returning to habitually.

What you say when you yell is not edited the way it would be in your calmer moments of conversation and discussion. The age-old "Think before you speak" is nearly impossible to apply when you are yelling—and if we look to the section on communication you may recall that what is said can never be taken back.

Most less successful parenting is based on impulse. The impulsive moves are about you feeling frustrated or over-excited, being in a rush, or feeling like there's nothing you can do—yet you have to do *something*. Impulsive responses often fail to positively change the situation or to reflect your personal values, and more often than not they make a situation worse. If you look at parenting as a journey, then this is about honking your horn in a traffic jam—short-term, impulsive, jarringly expressive and non-productive behavior that usually makes the drive unpleasant for you and for those around you.

> **REST AREA
> 1 MILE**
>
> How do I get my children to make their beds? Do their homework? Come home on time? Get off the phone? Get on the phone? (Yes, there is such a wish.) Turns out, in parenting, as in most relationships, managing others is ninety percent reliant upon first managing your own thoughts, feelings and behaviors.

Lessons about horn-honking are too often learned too late, when children have become young adults and are speaking up. At this point horn-honking parents find out that their impulsive moments made for a stormy climate that outweighed the finer moments of their parenting. Their children have forgotten a lot of the good times, and yet cannot forget those heated moments that were mismanaged. If the safety described early on in this book is to be put in place, yelling has to go.

Hitting the horn in a traffic jam really won't help, and just serves to prove that the one thing worse than a traffic jam is a noisy traffic jam.

About Change

In order to change a behavior, first address the frequency and intensity of the behavior. This is about aiming for better. To go from constant yelling to no yelling may be setting oneself up for failure. Allow yourself to move in stages, and take the time to recognize each successful moment when you avoid the habitual response. Your best parenting emerges when you rid yourselves of reactive responses and implement proactive strategies.

There are millions of these impulses and they happen in varying degrees from parent to parent, but everyone is honking the horn in some way, shape or form along the journey.

Which of these horns are you most likely to be leaning on?

Yelling

Nagging

Complaining

Bossing

Saying "right now"

Throwing stuff or yourself around

Threatening

Over-punishing

Being consistent and then losing it

Remember, if you want to stop any of your horn-honking impulses, start by identifying the reaction and deciding how often it is a problem. Honking the horn on an annual basis is different than doing it on a daily basis, and better means something different in either situation.

Aim for better. After you have a few successes with one thing and you are feeling encouraged, return to this list and see what you can address next. Rate yourself and your progress on a scale of frequency (I am doing this less and that feels good) or a scale of duration (I stopped myself early on and that feels good) or a scale of intensity of voice and actions (I really am calming down and the volume and tone are decreasing and that feels good).

Things I Can Do If I Find Out I'm Not Perfect

Just in case you've discovered you're not perfect, here are a few common problem-solvers for some of the horn-honking behaviors you are bumping into.

1. **Count:** Count to ten before doing or saying anything. *Anything.* Count in your head. Slowly. Buy the few extra seconds that make the difference between acting or speaking impulsively and considering the future goals for this relationship.

2. **Think First:** Try to adopt this as a new approach to acting impulsively. This is a thinking and planning exercise, not an emotional rollercoaster. Don't think only the moment before you speak; really set aside time to consider the challenges you face with horn-honking, and how you would like to change.

3. **Why Comes Later:** Stop the behavior first, *and then* work on not doing it again, *and then* figure out why you do it. Knowing why you yell has to come second: first, stop the yelling. Attempting to figure it out while it continues to happen is of little use. Figuring it out after it has stopped is very useful. Stopping is the most useful.

4. **Do Something Else:** Have a walk around the living room, the house, the block, the apartment floor or the yard. Walk around the whole town if you need to. Do something that is harmless and gets you away from the scene. Remove yourself

and do everyone (especially you) a favor until you can stay on the scene and not act out the impulse.

5. **Self-Talk:** Learn how to self-talk your way to safety. At times when the behavior(s) aren't frequent or about to take place, figure out what you need to tell yourself in order to retain control and decrease the frequency, intensity or duration.

6. **Set Up a Safety Station:** Set up a safety station in a private spot. Your safety station should include the things that help you relax or calm down, and help you recover so that you can re-enter the scene without resorting to behaviors that you don't like. Your safety station might include a favorite CD, your favorite flowers, a poem or story you enjoy, or notes about the steps you need to take to calm down. For example, at a private safety station you may find the following note to self:

> Take a deep breath.
>
> Think about relaxing.
>
> Throw some cold water on your face.
>
> Tell yourself out loud that you haven't blown it yet and you're not going to.
>
> Count to fifty looking at this postcard from our last holiday.
>
> Remember, you don't want to be your dad/ mom.
>
> Go back there and feel good.
>
> Come back if you need to.

Excuse yourself from the scene and head for your safety station. Return when your impulse has passed. Find a way to go back and feel good about not responding impulsively.

7. **Redirect:** Hum, hug, sing, laugh, whistle: do happy, expressive things to change the moment for yourself and everyone else. Inject humor into what was an escalating moment! Redirect your energy to change the flow, the direction and the obvious outcome.

8. **Change the Delivery:** Drop a note to one of the kids instead of using the usual (and expected and ignored) impulsive behavior. Leave a hint on the television at the end of the day. Text message and edit out the impulses before you send. Send a note with a gift. Trick yourself, challenge yourself, get the message across so that it works in the short term and has no long-term costs. Change the delivery, not the underlying parenting message that you would like to send in alliance with your children.

9. **Focus on Behaviors that Solicit Help:** Talk about how you are feeling to see if there's any support out there. For example, saying something like, "I feel like yelling and this doesn't feel great," will help to stop you from yelling, and it also lets others know that you are trying to change. Your statement will get both your family's attention and their assistance.

10. **Doing Nothing _Is_ Doing Something:** Try simply doing nothing. As simple as this sounds, be forewarned: doing nothing requires a lot of internal work when you are putting a behavioral change into motion.

    If you are co-parenting and you want to experiment with "doing nothing as doing something," you must let the co-parent know what you are up to.

To them it looks like you are not disciplining and not directing the children, but in fact, what you are doing is not yelling—an activity! As well, you are practicing not being impulsive and trying to be proactive. For the parent working at this, there is nothing worse than successfully managing your yelling habit for a full evening, only to have a co-parent come home and start yelling the moment he or she walks through the door. If doing nothing (to avoid doing something unhealthy) is going to work, make sure co-parents are in the loop!

It's tough to manage your own impulsive behavior, especially those impulses that seem to work in the short term. It's a long journey and you're in it for the long haul, so you need to have the strategy of self-management in place. One day at a time. Moment by moment.

The yell that never got yelled.

Chapter Thirty-Two

Friendly Advice About the Role of Friend

Many people wonder why I don't include the role of "friend" when talking about roles to use in parenting. There is a good reason. Just as your friends are not your parents, even when they are offering support or advice, it is not the role of the parent to be the child's friend. This sounds quite black and white and, of course, a gray area exists, but it is better to err on the side of caution than to get into the complexities that abound in this area of parenting. Parenting is a relationship, and all relationships require definition. In relationship terms, when the parent and child define themselves as friends, boundary issues arise that create confusion for both parent and child. The boundaries of the parent–child relationship are completely unlike those of the friend–friend relationship, and the confusion that can take place when the parent and the child are slipping and sliding back and forth from one to the other can have lasting negative effects on both parties.

At certain moments, when the support and encouragement of friendship is what the child wants, and something like a firm approach and a hard-line suggestion is what the child needs, the parent faces the conflict of dueling desires. The parent wants to do what is objectively necessary for their child, and also to champion the child as they would any friend. Whereas a friend is almost always certain to be "on one's side," the parent needs to maintain a boundary that will allow them to sustain their much-needed role as guide, teacher, caregiver, coach—and creator of boundaries. Mixing friendship with parenting limits the number of roles that parents can readily play without creating conflict.

Help your kids select and nurture great and lasting friendships of their own. Children have very few opportunities to find great parents, but they can find great friends in lots of places!

Keep in mind that your children are not your friends, either. If you find you are seeking their advice on adult matters, or your child ignores you in ways that suggest you are peers, or your child is the person you turn to for weekend plans or recreational activity, or your child continually behaves as co-parent of younger siblings, or your eldest says things like "you spend too much," echoing other adults in your life, it is time to use the role modeling strategy to choose more effective parenting roles.

Try redefining the framework of your parent–child relationship. Common phrases such as "my daughter and I are best friends," and "a great dad is a boy's best friend," sound fabulous to the listener; however, they are counter-productive. "My daughter and I are one heck of a great mother-daughter team," or "I'm always there for my son," will keep things in much less muddied waters. And clear waters mean fewer conflicts for parents and children alike. By rewriting these phrases, you can avoid confusion in the way you and your child see the relationship, and be better prepared for those rocky parent–child spots when the friendship thing has to go out the window in favor of other necessary roles.

Being the Friend To Avoid Upsets for Your child

Parents of children who don't have many friends find that not befriending their children becomes a difficult task. They find that over time they tend to become their children's friend in order to compensate for the absence of real friendships, and then changing their role to that of teacher or coach feels like abandoning the child. In fact, it is neither. Saving children from being alone while not dealing with their real dilemma of finding their own friends is no help at all! Children can learn from mistakes on the road to friendship—building social skills, trying out new and challenging social situations and lots more that the parent, as teacher, coach and guidance counselor can participate in fully.

Here is an example to clarify how being a friend is not helpful, as well as to show constructive ways to spend time with your children.

> Larissa can't find anyone to go to the movie with her on a Saturday afternoon. As it turns out, everyone has gone somewhere without her and she missed all the calls about the plans. In the end, none of her friends left her a message. With an open afternoon ahead, Larissa's mother decides to cancel her plans and go to the movie with Larissa. She says things like "C'mon, just us girls" to give it that "I'm your friend for this afternoon" feeling that she thinks will be helpful to Larissa. Larissa says okay (reluctantly) and off they go to the movie (a movie mom wouldn't see at any other time if her life depended on it!). Mom thinks all's well, until they run into Larissa's friends and they see Larissa at the same movie with her mother!

Like most children, Larissa's friendship dilemma comes down to the crossroads of inclusion or exclusion that can make or break a Saturday afternoon. Whether it is the neighborhood party or the afternoon at the movies, everyone feels good about being included and is hurt by the knowledge or experience of being excluded. In facing the experience of exclusion and the associated emotions, Larissa could have solved this one on her own and had the benefit of learning from the situation—but mom thought playing the role of friend might work.

The truth is, even if they hadn't seen Larissa's friends, this was not the movie to be at as a mother spending the day with her daughter. It would have been more helpful to Larissa if her mom had kept this a mother–daughter event. Larissa's mom could have simply said, "Let's go to a mother–daughter movie instead of one you and your friends would go to," and the great mother–daughter relationship would have surfaced.

It would have been most helpful if she had spent the time with Larissa as her mother, helping her come up with a solution to this predicament in the role of coach, teacher or guidance counselor. Larissa could have used suggestions about making plans earlier, encouragements to seek out other friendships, or support in efforts to confront her friends about being excluded. Mom can't choose the role of friend here and still be helpful in the more positive roles of teacher, listener, guidance counselor, coach and a host of others! Mom needs to accept that Larissa needs her as a parent in a helpful and supportive role, not as a peer. Mom can't be her friend here. Larissa has friends. They are out without her.

She needs a parent.

Chapter Thirty-Three

Changing the Tire and Calling the Auto Club

Realistic Decision-Making in the Age of Super Parents

Everyone who drives needs to learn how to change a flat tire. On the other hand, some of those same people, once they know how to change the tire, need to join the auto club and learn when they should call *them* to change the tire. For today's Super parent, the dilemma is no different. You have the wherewithal to do lots of things, but have difficulty knowing when to pass certain things along to others, let other things go or just take a break. For many of you, this is excruciatingly difficult!

REST AREA
1 MILE

Have you given yourself permission to take a break, ask for help, delegate to others, or, to let go of the Super mom or Super dad myth and to just do less?

Women of the past two decades have faced this challenge with the advent of the "Super mom" myth.

> She's a mom with three kids! She's a perfect wife and a dutiful daughter! She works full-time, and she's doing her MBA! She coaches Little League, she's a volunteer and she cares for an elderly neighbor! She's Super Mom! If only you were just like her, you too could pride yourself on doing the impossible and shooting for perfect!

Are you changing diapers, making dinner, studying and working full-time, and preoccupied by the need to have the laundry started before the weekend starts?

You need the auto club.

You need pizza delivery night (the food auto club).

You need a diaper service (the diaper version of the auto club).

Give yourself permission to use whatever it is that will help you along on this wild and demanding journey of parenting. Most of all, give yourself permission to stop and teach your children the following:

> *Everyone should know how to change a flat tire, and that sometimes you change the tire (because you have the time and energy to do this activity yourself), and sometimes you just call the auto club, turn in early, and save your energy for the more important parts of your life.*

As an off-shoot of the Super mom myth, the more recent "Super dad" myth has emerged.

He works a hundred hours a week and also cooks and cleans! He's the coach for select hockey and rep baseball! He reads two novels a week and speaks four languages! He takes little Susie to "Daddy and Me Class"! He took four months of paternity leave! He is carpool dad four days a week, gets up at 5:30 to work out and spends every weekend playing with his kids! He's Super dad!

At first it looked like the Super dad myth would bring men and women closer to being equal, but it worked the other way: they are spending more time apart. Both need to know when to make dinner and when to call for pizza.

Men will hopefully learn from women's experiences in this area of superhuman expectations. In fact, in today's world, co-parents, single parents, separated and divorced parents and step-parents all need to work on this together, no matter what their gender.

It is crucial to know how to do lots of things, but above all, know how to give yourself permission to give in. Not all the time. Just on busy nights.

Remember, this is your life. There's nothing to prove, and there is so much to enjoy! Use the support around you to enhance your family life and your personal well-being, and to buy yourself the much-deserved time you need to kick back with your loved ones. You created this marvelous, wild ride: do everything in your power to spend your precious life truly enjoying it. Just like treats and side trips, try not to miss out on the hidden pleasures of letting things go every once in a while.

Conclusion

The End of the Book, Not the End of the Journey

Writing a book about parenting is an act of hope.

At its most basic level, the hope is that you, the reader and parent, have taken in the ideas and practical suggestions about parenting and matched them with your own expertise to create a family in which better parenting is both the goal and the outcome.

My hope is that this book has offered you what it promised from the start: a perspective on how to look at family, rather than how a family should look. The value of being an expert on your own family and the perspective of aiming for better have been stressed in order to encourage you to continue on the parenting journey with confidence and with optimism. These two ideas—combined with the ideas for playing appropriate roles as a parent (such as teacher, coach or guide), working in alliance with and not in opposition to your children (and your co-parent!), using three words a day to keep things simple, and taking the Long View of parenting—will all help you find your way.

There's a great deal of value in planning for the parenting journey and this book is just one of the many resources you can gather for the trip. These are driver's manuals, and they are useful to have along on difficult and even not-so-difficult days on the road to better parenting. Parents of adult children tell us it never ends, that they parent their children even in their adult lives and that children (some of whom are forty and fifty years old) still need their parents' attention, and continue to make additional demands on their parents' energy—no matter how little energy they have left! The good news is that by this time in life the "thanks for . . . " and the other positives have usually started to flow, showing that appreciation and acknowledgement do come forward at op- portune moments when your children are adults. Your children's experiences of being parents themselves will enhance their ap- preciation of you as a parent more than you know. Keep parent- ing on the journey, the thank-you postcards are in the mail! It is immensely gratifying to raise adults, and then to have those adults a part of your life. Keep this in mind: think long.

The thread that runs through the book and through the journey is to aim for better. It works in parenting, and it can be a framework for the family itself to build on in order to begin to operate efficiently and co-operatively in the pursuit of happiness and success. It works for nuclear families and for step-families, single parents and step-parents, married and common-law couples, and for same-sex couples, too. Aiming for better works at times when things are really terrific and times when most strategies feel like rearranging the deck chairs on the *Titanic*. If there can be only one message you take with you after you close the covers and lay this book on your bedside table, let it be this one:

Aim for Better.

Index